AMERICA'S RAILROADS:

The Second Generation

Union Pacific's westbound *Omaha Express* (OEX) at Lawrence,
Kans., on August 18, 1975, with U50s #5033 and #5039. (BALL)

AMERICA'S RAILROADS:

The Second Generation

Don Ball, Jr.

W · W · NORTON & COMPANY
New York · London

TO MOM,

who not only trusted me on my own at a very young age, but would get me to a bus, or train, or ferry in order that I could spend the day at a roundhouse. She has always known my heart.

Without Whose Help

Support and *encouragement* are two durable terms that apply to those who have helped make this volume a reality. From tedious chores such as typing, to the furnishing of forgotten train numbers, many are to be thanked. First and foremost, my wife, Linda, who has let me turn the bedroom into a giant repository of notes and papers while writing this book, and who did the typing from my handwritten scribble. To Jim Boyd, who not only furnished the cream of his second-generation photos and the eloquent epilogue, but never gave up trying to educate me on diesels in the process. "You've got to groove on 'em, Don—steam is gone." And to T. J. (I call him Tom) Donahue who came up with so many of the beautiful shots that were needed to round out this book; Jim, T. J., and I all wishing we had another hundred pages "to really do it!"

Special thanks go to Bill Schaumburg for the beautiful photo-locator maps he prepared for each chapter (I *still* don't know what a 310 is, Bill), and to Jim Mairs of W. W. Norton & Company—one of those rare souls outside the railfan world who believed in this book from the outset. So, too, for the last-minute help from Jim's assistant, Marian Johnson, getting additional notes typed and inserted, etc., in the face of a deadline.

My most sincere thanks and appreciation go to Rich Snierson, Esq., and Bob Wells, Esq., who personally and professionally prodded me to complete the book in the face of obstacles.

Particular thanks go to Bernie Schleifer for the mechanical execution of this book and to Dick Wallin, who helped me locate those precious few original transparencies to complete the desired coverage. Appreciation also goes to Arnold Jospeh, who let me "browse at will" through his beautiful stock of annual reports and paper goods for those particular details I was researching.

Finally, there are several good friends who have made, and continue to make, my second-generation railfanning a lot more enjoyable; for this I am grateful. Walt Grosselfinger and Karl Wiemer, both with whom I have shared thousands of hours—from cabs to trackside, steam to diesel—pursuing trains. And to Don Sims, Joe Lucas, Joe McMillan, and Joe Collias (what is it about Joes and railroading?), who do their best to keep me on the right track. And last, but not least, Craig Willett, who is *still* looking to Walt and me for his rock.

The historical and technical information on which this book is based is drawn from books, papers, reports, and personal notes in my collection, and I assume responsibility for the content. Original transparencies in my collection are credited to the photographer whenever that information is known.

Published simultaneously in Canada by George J. McLeod Limited, Toronto.
Printed and bound by Dai Nippon Printing Co., Ltd., Tokyo, Japan.

Designed by Bernard Schleifer

FIRST EDITION

W. W. Norton & Company Inc. 500 Fifth Avenue New York N.Y. 10110
W. W. Norton & Company Ltd. 25 New Street Square London EC4A 3NT

ISBN 0 393 01416 9

1 2 3 4 5 6 7 8 9 0

CONTENTS

IN RETROSPECT...

THIS BOOK attempts to cover railroading in the '60s and '70s—from dieselization to Penn Central and Amtrak; Conrail to spin-off short-lines. Certainly these are two of the stormiest decades in history; twenty years of change have left many of us with spinning heads! In 1960, we had mainline steam. We had the Rutland, the New Haven, Central, and Pennsy. That same year General Electric jumped into the diesel-locomotive business with its high-horsepower U25B. Milwaukee's bipolar electrics were taken out of service while Burlington's *Pioneer Zephyr* was placed on permanent exhibition at Chicago's Museum of Science and Industry. It was in 1960 that Illinois Central added domes to passenger trains, while Seaboard experimented with passenger train–geared E7s on hotshots. Nineteen sixty pitted 2400 horsepower Alco DL600s against EMD's 2400 h.p. SD24. It was on February 21, 1960, that the Chicago North Shore & Milwaukee hauled 260 fans on a final salute to a railroad headed for total abandonment. In 1960, research began on prestressed concrete crossties on the ACL and SAL (we hadn't even thought of Seaboard Coast Line!). In 1960, the Pennsylvania took delivery of its first massive order of electric locomotives since receiving its last GG1s, while small Tennessee, Alabama & Georgia took delivery of the first diesel named after a living person—GP18 "Dave E. Hedges." And this is only the tip of the iceberg. In 1960, Union Pacific purchased Great Northern's huge 2-D + D-2 electric and hauled it back to Omaha to use it as the test bed for their coal-burning gas turbine locomotive; Southern Pacific and Rio Grande ordered German-built Krauss-Maffei diesel hydraulics, and Alco got into EMD's field of re-engining old diesels with the new 251-series engine. Incredibly, steamy Norfolk & Western took delivery of its 529th diesel unit and killed Roanoke steam forever, while already dieselized Illinois Central fired up several 4-8-2s and 2-10-2s to pitch in on surging coal traffic. Yes, if 1960 starts your head spinning, try the next 19 years!

Indeed, railroad events that made *headlines* in 1960, seemed unspectacular when compared to the changes that followed. Item: On May 1, 1960, the Southern Pacific ended its narrow-gauge history by ceasing operation of its 71-mile narrow-gauge Keeler Branch, while Milwaukee announced that it wanted to abandon 1½ miles of track between Prairie du Chien, Wis., and Marquette, Iowa, that crossed the Mississippi on a pair of pontoon bridges. Ex–Grand Trunk Western 0-8-0s went to work for Northwestern Steel & Wire in April 1960, as Santa Fe was completing its first CTC microwave-transmission installation. More newsworthy was the hyphen that appeared between Erie and Lackawanna, but that was to be expected. The news that Great Northern and Northern Pacific wanted a marriage that included the Burlington shook us a little, but this was the beginning of a new decade—one that would quickly temper us into accepting change.

Using the captions as a "running text," I have tried to cover chronologically

20 years, commencing with 1960, while adhering to the usual geographic path. This has not been easy, considering the years in retrospect and how they tumbled after one another full of stunning—really unbelievable—events. In places, compromise has been sought between history's fast-moving chronology of events and geographic coverage, subject matter and space limitations— I hope with a degree of success. Consider, if you will, the implications of starting a book at a period when the J. G. White Engineering Corporation was being retained to study the merger of the Boston & Maine, Rutland, Maine Central, Bangor & Aroostook, New Haven, and Boston & Albany railroads. Consider, too, ending the same book (maybe I should say first chapter) sans three of the above railroads. Consider also the interim creation of Penn Central, Conrail, Amtrak, MBTA, Vermont Railway, and Green Mountain Railroad—and I'm now only talking about New England! And then there's born-again Providence & Worcester Railroad, asleep as a nonoperating company since 1880, suddenly coming back to life and taking on Conrail in New England yet! It's fashionable to neatly package or label decades and their events with descriptive slogans such as "the roaring twenties"; I'd label the railroad events of the '60s and '70s "astounding!" In earlier decades, trains and engines changed, but for the most part, not much else. As we photographed engines and trains in the '60s and '70s, *entire railroads* were disappearing.

Looking back, the '60s and '70s have not been happy decades. The creation of Penn Central and the agonizing feeling that many of us had over the slim chances of it succeeding is something I cannot forget. The continuing series of melodramatic threats to shut down all service until the government put enough money into the railroad's bottomless tin cup to permit it to meet its next payroll were bleak days of black paint and red ink, days we helplessly wanted to put an end to. For lawyers and consultants, the steady erosion guaranteed fees and provided employment, and this was the bright side!

No, we seem to have lost sight of what truly drives our economy and what is required to keep our nation's products and services competitive in world markets. Worse, our vision of the future appears to have narrowed to include only that which is fashionable politically and expedient for the short term. Today, the solvent Providence & Worcester is offering to restore rail-freight service in southern New England over what are now Conrail lines, to be operated in the private sector. Conrail is fighting P&W on this, but at the same time is publicly asking: "How are the needs of the rail industry going to be paid for?" I, as taxpayer, author, and American, feel that I have to speak out. If, as a nation, we are unable to revitalize our productive capacity, we will pay the price. And it's a price, I feel, we need not, and should not, have to pay. The problems are daunting. Even our way of life, as well as security, is threatened. This is the time for self-questioning and, perhaps, planning for *our* very survival.

In retrospect, I relish the fact that I can still open this book on mainline steam operations. In truth, by 1960, the diesel's oily smell of death had permeated every class 1 railroad in North America, but in Canada, the Canadian Pacific continued to operate in the *grand tradition*, almost defying time. Nineteen fifty-nine was the moment of reckoning for mainline steam operations in the United States. The few major railroads that operated steam in 1960 are pictured in this book. In July 1959, the Union Pacific fired up eight Challengers and seven Big Boys to haul grain and fruit during the harvest, but that was it. Duluth, Missabi & Iron Range was operating its huge Yellowstones in 1959, but along came a steel strike. Nickel Plate operated a few 0-8-0s in its Conneaut yard in '59, but the steel strike sealed the fate of the ready-to-roll Berkshires. Norfolk & Western continued to operate some Y-6 mallets on mine runs, but the diesel replacements were en route. The message was clear.

Perhaps the best steam show in the United States in 1959 was Grand Trunk Western—offering up a fine display of steam-powered freights, through passenger runs, and commuter trains.

Nineteen sixty threatened my interest in the railroad scene. Everything had changed in railroading, including my love for it. What I did not realize at the time—or for years to come—was that we *still* had steam-era railroading into the '60s. Sure, the motive power changed, but for the most part, the diesels that ran were born in the steam era, and were the *very survivors* that had battled with steam. Like banners of triumph, they rolled across divisions, emblazoned in their decorative colors! At EMD, GE and Alco, the mechanical engineers and designers were looking at railroading in a far different light: SD24s, GP20s, U25Bs, and Century series second-generation diesels were moving off the drafting tables and onto the production line. Those same diesels that survived into the '60s would soon be on their way toward extinction. Indeed, all of the steam-era diesels were to become "targets" for trade-in offers on the new breed of diesels.

I was wrong in my quick assessment that with the demise of steam, railroading had both completely changed and had lost all of its glamor. The images in this book bear testimony to the fact. A candy-apple red Alco RS3 burbling through the lush Vermont back country . . . a new Rock Island Geep flying across the flatness of Kansas in winter . . . the absolute elegance of an Illinois Central E-unit . . . the timeless Santa Fe warbonnets on the move . . . three noisy Alco Century 425s heading a Lehigh Valley hotshot . . . Espee's angular, almost menacing looking, SD45 bursting into sunlight . . . UP's huge yellow double-engined diesels rolling through endless country—and still looking huge . . .North Western's Baby Train Masters lugging ore . . . New York Central's GP7-Alco lash up, on the rampage with coal . . . and Rio Grande's EMDs sprinting freight over the Rockies. No, railroading is still exciting, and I have a feeling that as long as we're talking steel-flanged wheels on steel rails, it will remain so.

T. J. DONAHUE:
A SELF-INTRODUCTION

I WAS A CHILD of the steam era, literally and emotionally, and when, with the triumph of the diesel, that era neared its end, I avidly sought out the last of steam. For me, in the middle and late '50s, that meant the Big Boys on Sherman Hill, K4s at South Amboy, CV power in my own Connecticut, the Rio Grande narrow gauge, the Grand Trunk and Grand Trunk Western, the Boston & Maine, the DM&IR, the BC&G, and Canada, Canada, Canada! If at home for the steam fan it was the Twilight of the Gods, then Canada, with its bustling steam activity, was like life after death. Many a time, after working the third or graveyard shift at Burr Road Tower, I would drive some 369 miles to Montreal, arriving at Dorval in time for the evening commuter rush, spend the next day and the morning of the third day between Dorval and Vaudreuil where the CPR and CNR mains ran so conveniently side by side, then drive back home, arriving in time to go back to work! Such was my devotion to steam, and I know that others far exceeded me in ardor.

But the end was in sight, and, meanwhile, there were the diesels, not only in the wings, but on stage. What to do? Should I emulate some of my peers and, like the jilted Miss Havisham of Dickens' *Great Expectations*, retire into wounded seclusion? But railroading was to me more than locomotives—it was the B&O high iron with dressed stone ballast, it was NYNH&H upper-quadrant semaphores bowing reverently to the passing *Merchants Limited*, it was the multiple slip switches of South Station, and the elegant signal gantries of the New York Central with their approach lighting, that enabled a fan to loll at his ease until the double green flashed on. It was the PRR's electrified main line, fearsome with hurtling GG1s and their imperious air horns, and the long corridor of ranked New Haven lacework catenary bridges, as classical as ancient Rome. It was Nicholson Viaduct, and Tunnel No. 1 at Plainview, Col.; it was Horseshoe Curve, and Santa Margarita Pass, and Hell Gate. And, as Thomas Wolfe wrote, it was the "demon hawkeye of the rails with gloved hand of cunning," and a goggled fireman sighting down the left side of an I5 for signals, and a dignified conductor critically examining his gold Railway Special before waving a highball—all this and more was bound up in my passion for trains. So I made my peace with the diesels. Initially, I ignored them, then tolerated them, and then learned to like them. Taken out of context, they couldn't compare with steam, but set down in their native habitat, they could be impressive, dramatic, and, above all, colorful.

By way of example, the *Denver Zephyr* making a station stop and engine-crew change at Ottumwa, Iowa, on a quiet fall evening, the big silver Es idling passively while the new crew climbs aboard, the engineman settling himself comfortably in his seat, then the radio-borne highball, and the oscillating headlight flashes on—a dramatic prelude to the pure theater to follow. The idling shifts to that native EMD chant where the Es seem to accelerate in place; then, the sleek silver Limited is moving, sliding past, a last vestibule door slamming, a peremptory blast of the horn at some unoffending crossing, and the oscillating red Mars light on the rear slashing across the rails like some bloody mark of Zorro!

The diesel is finally vindicated though at Cajon Pass, that happy hunting ground in the Mojave Desert, where the Santa Fe, UP and SP daily present the Greatest Show on Earth. It's a cast of consummate actors—the Santa Fe a dashing Beau Brummel of the rails, matching its blue, yellow, and red to the pastels of the desert—the giant yellow UP, urbane and powerful, and the sober SP, dogged and relentless.

It must have been great there in steam days, but not much more so!

1
YANKEE SPIRIT

AMTRAK
BANGOR AND AROOSTOOK RAILROAD CO.
BELFAST & MOOSEHEAD LAKE RAILROAD CO.
BOSTON AND MAINE RAILROAD
CANADIAN NATIONAL RAILWAYS
CANADIAN PACIFIC RAILWAY
CENTRAL VERMONT RAILWAY, INC.
CLAREMONT AND CONCORD RAILWAY CO.
CONNECTICUT DEPARTMENT OF TRANSPORTATION
GREEN MOUNTAIN RAILROAD CORP.
LAMOILLE VALLEY RAILWAY
LONG ISLAND RAIL ROAD CO.
MAINE CENTRAL RAILROAD CO.
MASSACHUSETTS BAY TRANSPORTATION AUTHORITY
NEW YORK, NEW HAVEN AND HARTFORD RAILROAD CO.
PENN CENTRAL TRANSPORTATION CO.
PROVIDENCE AND WORCESTER CO.
ST. JOHNSBURY & LAMOILLE COUNTY RAILROAD
SPRINGFIELD TERMINAL RAILWAY CO.
STEAMTOWN FOUNDATION
THE VALLEY RAILROAD CO.
VERMONT RAILWAY, INC.

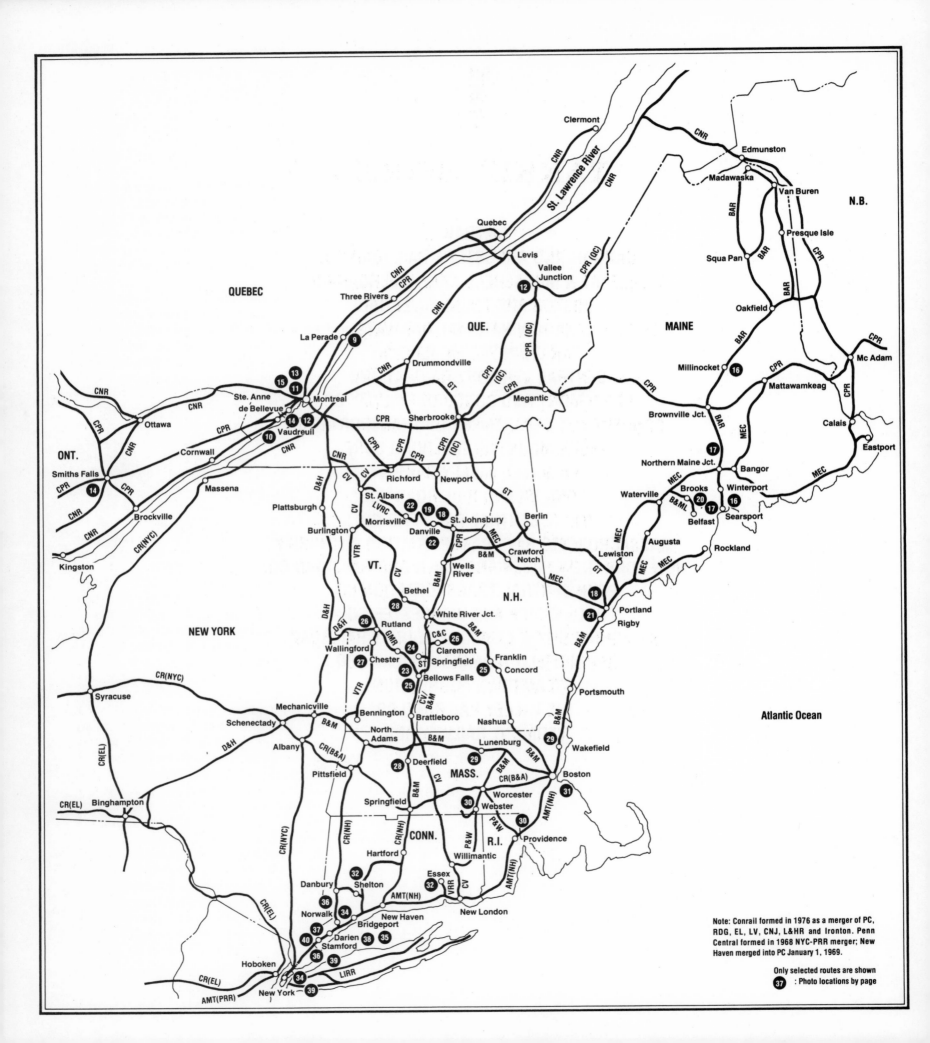

Clermont

CNR

Edmunston

N.B.

Madawaska

Van Buren

BAR

Presque Isle

BAR

Squa Pan

BAR

CPR

St. Lawrence River

CNR

CNR

Quebec

CPR (QC)

MAINE

Oakfield

Levis

Vallee Junction

12

QUE.

CPR

Mc Adam

Three Rivers

CNR

CPR

CPR (QC)

Millinocket

16

CPR

QUEBEC

CNR

CPR (QC)

Mattawamkeag

CPR

La Perade

9

Drummondville

CPR (QC)

Megantic

Brownville Jct.

BAR

Calais

13

GT

CPR (QC)

Northern Maine Jct.

17

15

11

Montreal

CNR

Sherbrooke

CPR

MEC

Bangor

Eastport

Ste. Anne de Bellevue

CNR

CPR

CPR

CPR

GT

MEC

14 12

CPR

CPR

CPR (QC)

ONT.

Ottawa

CPR

10

Vaudreuil

CNR

CNR

Richford

Newport

GT

MEC

Waterville

Brooks

20

17

Winterport

Smiths Falls

Cornwall

CNR

CV

CV

St. Albans

MEC

B&ML

16

CPR

14

CPR

Massena

D&H

LVRC

22

19

18

St. Johnsbury

Berlin

MEC

Belfast

Searsport

CPR

CNR

Plattsburgh

CV

Morrisville

Danville

CPR

B&M

MEC

Augusta

Brockville

CNR

Burlington

22

Crawford Notch

Lewiston

MEC

Rockland

CR(NYC)

VTR

VT.

Wells River

GT

MEC

MEC

Kingston

CV

Bethel

N.H.

MEC

18

D&H

28

White River Jct.

B&M

21

Portland

NEW YORK

26

Rutland

B&M

Rigby

D&H

Wallingford

GMR

24

C&C

26

Claremont

B&M

CR(NYC)

27

Chester

ST

Springfield

Franklin

Syracuse

VTR

23

25

Bellows Falls

25

Concord

Mechanicville

25

CV

B&M

Portsmouth

Bennington

Brattleboro

Nashua

B&M

Schenectady

B&M

29

Wakefield

D&H

North Adams

B&M

Lunenburg

CR(EL)

Albany

CR(B&A)

29

Binghampton

Pittsfield

28

Deerfield

MASS.

B&M

CR(EL)

CV

Boston

31

CR(NYC)

B&M

Worcester

CR(B&A)

Springfield

30

Webster

CR(NH)

CR(NH)

30

AMT(NH)

CONN.

P&W

Providence

Hartford

R.I.

CR(NYC)

32

Willimantic

AMT(NH)

Danbury

Shelton

Essex

CR(EL)

36

New Haven

32

VRR

CV

34

Bridgeport

AMT(NH)

New London

37

38

35

Hoboken

40

Darien Stamford

CR(EL)

36

39

34

LIRR

AMT(PRR)

New York

39

Atlantic Ocean

Note: Conrail formed in 1976 as a merger of PC, RDG, EL, LV, CNJ, L&HR and Ironton. Penn Central formed in 1968 NYC-PRR merger; New Haven merged into PC January 1, 1969.

Only selected routes are shown

37 : Photo locations by page

I N A 1912 story, the *New York Daily–Tribune* commented on the waves of immigrants coming to America: "The Yankee is Disappearing as Foreign Hordes Overrun New England. The Legendary Nasal Twang is Drowned in a Babel of Strange European Tongues." The native's only hope was "May these newcomers, with their peasant brawn and eager ambitions, employ the heritage the real New Englander has left, to become American in the truest sense."

Although much of the steadiness ascribed to the original Yankee character may be gone, I think the immigrants may have done the original Yankees one better, holding on to the values of hard work, self-reliance, and stability, while evincing hostility toward the very changes that have buffeted our land everywhere else. (In my town, we have a Holiday Inn—but it does not look like one. The sign is an 8-inch-in-height, 4-feet-across wooden one, painted green with "Holiday Inn" neatly spelled out in white script.) The modern Yankee, like his ancestor, disapproves of extremes; the land of Steady Habits is no idle label. Yankees are often kidded about their thrift, too, but I see an underlying thread of individual responsibility in this New England. Rather than priding itself on generosity to outsiders or in the erection of glorious public buildings—or awaiting massive government expenditures to keep things going— the Yankee Spirit reflects a hard-working steadiness, despite change elsewhere.

The Boston & Maine pioneered internal-combustion motive power back in 1924, operating a General Electric/Ingersoll-Rand oil-electric locomotive in test service for a period of time, but it was not until a decade later that the railroad purchased such a locomotive. In 1943 and 1944, the B&M bought six 4-unit FT diesel freighters to help unclog their war-swollen railroad, but it was not until 1954 that management decided to replace their fit, but antique, 4-4-0s and 2-6-0s in commuter service with 10 Alco RS3 diesels. In 1957, the B&M finally ordered 50 GP9s to phase out steam. During the next 10 to 15 years, most railroads were "redieselizing" with the new higher horsepower second-generation diesels; not so on the B&M. Those 50 engines were mechanically sound and did the job. In 1973, the first second-generation diesels were delivered to the B&M—12 new EMD GP38-2s.

The story is very much the same on the Central Vermont, which took delivery of a pair of Alco diesel switchers in 1941, but made do with what it had until two RS3s were ordered in 1954, followed by 18 GP9s from EMD in 1956–1957. During the next two decades, the GP9s remained the backbone of the Central Vermont's locomotive fleet. In 1977, 10 Alco RS11s from affiliated Duluth, Winnipeg & Pacific joined the GP9s in a swap of engines that left CV with 11 of its own GP9s, five GP9s from affiliate Grand Trunk Western, and the 10 RS11s. With the exception of SW1200 #1511, all of CV's present fleet of engines is well over 20 years old—and running just fine, thank you.

On the Bangor and Aroostook—another New England railroad, frugal and unconcerned with style—the story is very much the same. Many of the BAR's mainline diesels have been on the job now for over 30 years. I view this as a sure sign that, despite constant change elsewhere, the new Yankees have not strayed far from where they began. And what about the "new" Providence & Worcester? In February 1973, at the ceremony marking the re-birth of the P&W, Penn Central's New England region vice president, William H. Tucker, told P&W's president, Robert Eder, "You have a solvent railroad—at least for today." *Today*, as I write this, Yankee Providence & Worcester is alive, well, and thriving!

In my book, today's Yankee still shows the determination to survive through self-reliance—something we call Yankee Spirit.

Since this first chapter deals with New England, let me draw a parallel that will help chronicle the railroad scene during the '60s and '70s. Most Americans, and foreign visitors, view America in terms of the gargantuan dimensions of which Thomas Wolfe wrote: *the Grand Canyon, the mighty Rockies, the vast wheat fields, the grand Pacific Redwoods, the towering skyscrapers of New York City.* Grand images of a vast country. And yet, New England, while quite the opposite in scale, is a microcosm of mountains and rivers, tiny farms, diminutive villages, and quite large cities. Travelers often find themselves winding over narrow roads in miniature, rural Currier and Ives scenes that they can be a part of. New England quickly brings our history into perspective. When and where change did occur in *my* New England experience it was with Penn Central—almost as though it *invaded* New England! The New Haven sets the scene.

In 1960, I was a regular rider of the New Haven, and I feel as though I became a part of the New Haven family. During this time the New Haven was under the tight-working trusteeship of Messrs. Smith, Kirk, and Dorigan. It was a period of rebuilding, improving—fighting to stay alive. The New Haven was taking delivery of its new FL9 locomotives to eliminate engine changes at New Haven. At the same time, major improvements were being made in the New York–Boston and New York–Springfield schedules with savings of 27 minutes in running time. The railroad advertised that it would fight and spend to get more passengers. Nineteen sixty saw the introduction of new mechanized maintenance-of-way machines and the implementation of a major road-bed improvement program. An ambitious CTC installation was begun in 1960 on the Maybrook freight line at the same time that President Alpert launched a hard drive to boost 1960 freight revenues to $90 million. Plans for a new electronic freight yard at Cedar Hill were unveiled, with Charles E. Ragland, vice-president—freight traffic, stressing that the new facility would help speed freight through that terminal. Executive vice-president Shannon told the freight sales force: "In 1960, we will be able to give you men a really top-notch service that you will be proud to sell." Proof of the pudding came with the inauguration of the nation's hottest freight train, the *Yankee Jet*, between Boston and Chicago. At the same time, an all-out drive to increase piggyback business was started, with the purchase of new tractors and trailers and the speed-up of schedules in the face of growing highway diversion. In 1960, the New Haven set its sights high with an intensified industrial-development program. Indeed, in 1960 one could walk into the spacious New Haven R.R. Travel Bureau in the main waiting room of Grand Central Terminal and pick up some of the most beautiful and striking full-color brochures and post cards of "New Haven's New England" and the trains that served the region. I have saved an elegant New Haven folder that opens up to 28 inches across, the first double-page color spread showing the great Atlantic breakers rolling into a jagged coastline. Quoting the tastefully overprinted copy written by John McNulty, "There are some people who know all about those lovely old white doorways, and there are some others who know all about the Indians around Massachusetts and Rhode Island two or three hundred years ago. Still others know all there is to know about Paul Revere and Roger Williams, and there are some who have great knowledge of lobsters and of keen, swift sailing boats that skim a-tilt over Narragansett Bay and off Marblehead. There is none of these things that I know all about. I'm thinking of them, though. Because I'm sitting in the dining car of the New York to Boston train, having a cup of tea, looking out the window near Kingston, Rhode Island, and I'm feeling happy and content because I'm going to New England for a visit." I'd like to add—I know how he feels! That was 1960.

During the next two years, with the completion of the parallel New England Thruway, the New Haven found itself fighting for its very survival. In 1963, the line purchased the 12 Virginian Railway EF-4 ignatron freight electric locomotives—casualties of the N&W merger and dieselization—at an unbelievable $25,000 per unit. With recent dissatisfaction of the diesel's performance under the wires, 11 of the "Virginians" were shopped on a priority program and rushed into mainline freight service; the 12th unit was wisely set aside for parts. Those of us at trackside shared sentiments with the Operating Department (though for different reasons, perhaps) and were delighted to see this "de-dieselization" take place. Rumors abounded that more "used" electrics would be coming—even Virginian's huge GE double-unit streamliners that rode on 36 wheels and developed over 6,000 horsepower but couldn't duck under certain clearances of New Haven. We heard that all remaining New Haven freight electrics that were long out of service would be rebuilt. These wonderful things did not happen, but dreaming was fun, while we could. For the most part, New Haven did a fine job of making do with what it had, and those "Virginians," without a doubt, were the best investment in motive power in the 20 years that this book covers.

Penn Central . . . it's hard to keep a civil tongue! When I was in grade school, I knew a real goop who, like me, loved trains and had an extensive layout in his basement. He loved both the New York Central and the Pennsylvania and found it hard to compatibly model both. Nevertheless, he went ahead incorporating both roads and even had his dad make up some passes for his railroad. Without much imagination, he named the road Penn Central.

While the New Haven was busy piggybacking and pleasing passengers, though admittedly fighting for cash, the *big* Penn Central, merging the New York Central System and the Pennsylvania Railroad, was born at 12:01 A.M on February 1, 1968. At the 30th Street Station in Philadelphia, car foreman John McMurrough walked up to a private business car lettered *Central* and stripped off a sheet of paper concealing the word *Penn*, which had been painted in advance for this momentous occasion. Closer to home—and to the New Haven—New York building superintendent Warren R. Grove and two carpenters hung a PC banner over the main staircase at GCT. Grove proclaimed: "Now, it's official." Next step was the commencement of passing out *Call Us Penn Central* buttons to the far-flung family of almost 100,000 men and women. The day's papers and television featured the PC logo and its story as told by William A. Lashley, vice-president of public relations and advertising: "This symbol is designed to give a feeling of both strength and modernity. It suggests forward motion—a company on the go. It's simple, but distinctive—the symbol gives immediate identification and is easily remembered. We believe that it effectively expresses the dynamic quality of this exciting and challenging new enterprise we call the Penn Central." Sic Transit Nausea. . . .

Precisely at 11:59 P.M. on December 31, 1968, the New Haven became a part of Penn Central and the large green PC banner flew over the former general offices at 54 Meadow Street, New Haven. Happy New Year! Immediately, changes started to take place on the now ex–New Haven (and believe me, here's where another book should be written!). That very New Year's Day, train service between New York and Boston dropped from 27 to 16 trains. The EP-5 class ignatron electrics were downgraded to GCT commuter train service as PRR and PC painted GG1s stormed over Hell Gate Bridge and onto the ex–New Haven. Silverliners and Jersey Arrow commuter cars came, too—on test runs. Passing in the opposite direction went the distinctive and successful Virginian electrics, to work Pennsy tonnage (even after the merger of NYC and PRR, the merged railroad was called Pennsy—maybe for obvious reasons). One week after the inclusion of New Haven into PC, Stuart T. Saunders, chairman of Penn Central, held a press conference in Boston to address the future of rail freight service in New England. Saunders gave a hint of management thinking when he said, "Penn Central, henceforth, will pay a great deal more attention to its trucking subsidiary, New England Transportation Company."

I was commuting on the dear old New Haven during the takeover ("rape" is what the New Haven folks called it), and the PC innovations and changes were instant. The flow of freight service was turned upside down with everything being rerouted up through the ex-NYC Selkirk Yard—taking 48 hours longer running time into New England from Potomac Yard than over the L&HR–Maybrook Bridge route. The January snow swirled, and trains would often be canceled or annulled—something that never happened on the New Haven. Our nice reclining seat 8600 series day coaches were modified so that half the seats faced one way and half the other way—and, of course, no longer reclined. PRR P-70s and even older New York Central standard coaches bumped the newer New Haven cars. MU trains of old equipment not seen in a decade east of Stamford reappeared. Oh, yes, the NH curtains came out of the bar cars, which now charged "new prices" for their libations and more spartan surroundings. On the outside of the cars, plastic *Penn Central* and PC letterboards and logos were riveted over the stainless steel *New Haven* letterboards and logos. The New Haven McGinnis red was replaced with the PC pea-soup green. As far as locomotives go, the first EP-5 jet to be shopped merely received a single coat of PC blackwash with white worms over an unsandblasted surface. That was in May 1970. In April 1973, two years after Amtrak had taken over the long-distance trains, the new M-2 Cosmopolitan cars arrived, sans leg room, but painted McGinnis red and lettered New Haven for PC's New Haven Line. The new cars spelled doom for all of the ex-NH stainless steel MUs. At night, now, I hear the brash horns of the M-2s heading through the woods and over the numerous grade crossings on the New Canaan line, but up until 1973, the soft, distant Hancock whistles of the former New Haven cars were a comforting sound and a pleasure to listen to, especially in the wee small hours.

Penn Central provided lots of ammunition for jokes and criticism from its now ex–New Haven employees. In addition to its cloak of black for the NH, there were general orders upon general orders—replacing yesterday's general order that superceded the GO from the day before. Soon, "lick 'em–stick 'ems" were devised, so general orders could merely be licked and stuck over the previous one. The first PC employee timetable that was issued for every employee to carry while on duty forgot one thing—train schedules. A general order, accompanied by public timetables, rectified the problem. After a couple of years of general orders, bulletins, lick 'em–stick 'ems, vital moments, buttons, green doo-dads, and the like from the papercrats in Philadelphia, the Pennsy rules examiners concurred that the ex–New Haven could get trains over the road by simply "operating as usual."

Now, one final look at a bit of Yankee Spirit. Don Sims and I were up in Maine looking over the Maine Central and the Belfast and Moosehead Lake. One night we found ourselves stuck in a motel on the outskirts of town, where we had considerable difficulty finding something to do after the sun went down. We eventually won the confidence of a native at a nearby bar. Sims popped the question: "Hey, fella, where's the action?" The fella nodded conspiratorially, knowing exactly what was on Don's mind, and took him "to this place, aya, where they go clammin' illegally."

What better way to open up this volume than by showing Canadian National and Canadian Pacific steam in its final, and perhaps finest, hour, closing out the decade of the '50s! Canadian National was good housekeeping, impressive; Canadian Pacific was elegance. Canadian National *is* government owned; Canadian Pacific private enterprise. Both are the largest railroads in the Western Hemisphere, and the competition between the two is tough; neck and neck across the continent.

Something to ponder. From 1941 to January 1959, the privately owned Canadian Pacific paid its stockholders $368 million in dividends, and paid income taxes amounting to $348 million to the Canadian government. In this same period, Canadian National paid no taxes. And in these 18 years the CPR earned a profit of $669 million while the CNR suffered a loss of $653 million.

Ledger sheets and thoughts of government versus private ownership are quickly buried by the stride of CNR's high-stepping Pacific #5257 on train No. 172 heading past Guelph, Ont., on its Owen Sound to Toronto trek. And what about Canadian Pacific's magnificent standard Hudson #2818 highballing freight eastbound at LaPerade, Que. Was the world ever so right? (DONAHUE, BALL)

When it comes to the two Canadian roads and possibly favoring one over the other, I just let pictures speak for themselves. And speak they do, as we watch Canadian Pacific's semi-streamlined G3 Pacific #2459 accelerate train No. 272 from Vaudreuil, Que., across the placid waters of the St. Lawrence River onto Île Perrot on its morning run to Montreal. And how about that CPR Royal Hudson (above) tiptoeing her 12,000 imperial gallons of water and 21 tons of coal through the leads out of Glen Yard, heading (rather, backing) toward her waiting train in Windsor Station. The smart set of Budd cars—flying green flags yet!—speak well for themselves too, approaching Montreal West, as train No. 8 first section, en route into Windsor Station. On the Canadian Pacific, the Budd cars are called *Dayliners*—auto-rail Diesel climatized. Why did I say I had a favorite? (DONAHUE)

Above, one of Quebec Central's tidy 4-6-2s performs for us against the picturesque rural Quebec countryside ne Vallee Jct., Que., heading the westbound mixed toward Sherbrooke and a important connection with parent Canadian Pacific. At left, 1960 is more o less abruptly ushered upon us with th intrusion of Canadian National F7 die sels crossing over from CPR to CNR rails at Dorval, the fireman grabbing orders on the fly. At upper right, Cana dian Pacific's A1e class 4-4-0 #29 slow her 71-year journey (that's right, she was built in 1887!) to take on water at Perry, N.B., on her meandering way to Norton. The line's 65- and 75-pound rails and three bridges with light axle loadings were the reasons for the continued operation of three ancient 4-4-0 along the 44.6-mile branch between Norton and Chipman. Alas, in 1960, a lightweight diesel arrived, putting an end to these delightful shenanigans. I November 1960 #29 made a farewell trip that included a 75th-anniversary re-enactment of the driving of CP's las spike completing the transcontinental route across Canada. At lower right, CPR's #2397 hurries out her career o an eastbound commuter train near Westmount, Que., in January 1960. (DONAHUE)

By happy circumstance, as the preceding sampling of pictures show, the glorious age of steam along the Canadian Pacific lasted clear through the decade of the '50s and into 1960. When dieselization did occur, almost mercifully, the sweep of assignments by the diesels took place practically overnight. At upper left, one of the last Hudsons to operate, #2811, is captured by the camera on May 1, 1960, approaching the old railroad town of Smith Falls, Que., with a farewell excursion sponsored by the Canadian Railroad Historical Society. At immediate left, and quite typical of the "post 2-8-2 freight" along the CPR, an American-built FA1 teams up with an RS3 on westbound merchandise across the spans at Ste. Anne de Bellevue, Que., in May of 1960. Above, train No. 8, *The Dominion*, clicks along eastward toward Montreal, through Montreal West behind FP7 diesels in the summer of 1960. Thankfully, Canadian Pacific did not lose its Beaver with the arrival of the diesels. Returning to the 2811, she covered the return 128.7-mile trip to Montreal in 130 minutes, making four stops and one heavy reduction! The pleasure of the above-90-mph running was tempered only by the fact that she had recently lost her status on the active roster. (DONAHUE)

With almost exclusive domain over the entire eastern half of the state of Maine, it's little wonder that the modest-sized Bangor and Aroostook exhibits an independent Yankee spirit. At a time when other roads literally run their locomotives "into the ground" and then trade them in for new models, the BAR has used its seasonal lulls to keep its motive power in excellent repair. Consequently, roughly one-third of today's fleet is over 30 years old—and 15 years is considered a normal economic life elsewhere for a diesel! Wearing builder's plates dating 1948 and 1949, an F3 and two rare BL2 road switchers (left) rumble over a trestle near Winterport, Me., with the northbound leg of the Searsport job on October 12, 1976, with a trainload of empty potato refrigerators and jumbo tank cars of fuel oil bound for the power plants of the paper mills around Millinocket. Later that same evening, F3 #45 (below left) idles briefly in the Millinocket engine terminal before moving out as part of the locomotive consist that will pull freight No. 28 south to Northern Maine Junction. This classic 1948-built cab unit is known as a "chicken wire" F3 because of the distinctive screening over its side air intake grilles. And that jaunty bell over the cab windows is a unique BAR touch.

   Although much more youthful in appearance, GP7s 70 and 71 date back to 1950. #71 (right) is viewed moving about in the engine terminal at Northern Maine Junction west of Bangor in September 1978, as sister engine 70 (below) was laying over at Searsport on October 14, 1976. More BAR frugality: that red buggy on the odd trucks is a rebuilt World War II troop sleeper! (*No. 71*, BALL; *all others,* BOYD)

Although the white flags identify it as "Extra 5543 North," this train is known on the Grand Trunk out of Portland, Me., as No. 393, the morning hotshot to Montreal. Only a few miles out of Portland's waterfront yard, the three Canadian National GP38-2s and a GT GP9 have the merchandise rolling about 50 mph. Of all the CN's U.S. subsidiaries, New England's GT has come closest to losing its identity in both motive power and operations.

The Maine Central got the Bicentennial spirit in a big way, and instead of just painting up one red, white, and blue unit, it designated its ten new General Electric U18Bs delivered in May 1975 as the "Independence Class," and gave them golden eagles on their short hoods. In addition, each unit was named after a significant patriot or event. On an October midnight in 1976, MEC #403, *General Peleg Wadsworth*, is reflected in a rain pool in St. Johnsbury, Vt., as it pauses for an air test before departing for Crawford Notch and Portland with freight YR-1.

The schedule for YR-1 had changed by October 1978, and the train was making its run through Crawford Notch, N.H., in the morning daylight. Since this was a regular assignment for the Independence Class U18Bs, I was eager to catch a consist of the handsome eagle-emblazoned units in fall colors—in spite of a drizzling rain and 1/250th at f2 exposure. At once the descending train is heard, approaching my trackside location near Notchland, and what is on the point—a grubby old red unit leading an old green one! Kiss the gold engines good-by! I was furious at the time, but wouldn't you know, Jim saw the shot and said "I've been trying to get a red Geep in the lead around there for years and you just stumble into it...." (BOYD, BOYD, BALL)

Much of the Yankee charm of New England is manifested in the daily comings and goings of its numerous "little trains" operating on uncertain rail that barely supports today's high-cube cars. The Belfast & Moosehead Lake Railroad's daily train from the Maine Central interchange at Burnam Jct., Me., plies along through meadows near Brooks, Me., the 60-pound rail noticeably bending under the covered hopper's 263,000-lb. gross-on-the-rail. I was "chasing" this train with friend and photographer Don Sims, when in the progress of pacing he stopped the car to change film. Much to my delight, I discovered I could keep up with the train— on foot! #50 is a 1946 GE 70-ton diesel. The 33.07-mile line to Belfast Harbor was chartered on February 28, 1867, and began operations on August 1, 1868. Our encounter was on August 31, 1978. On the right, two studies of Boston & Maine second-generation power at Rigby Yard, Portland, on September 1, 1978. The implications go way beyond the new paint scheme, named diesels and "implied solitude" of the two photos.

By year's end, 1973, 12 new EMD GP38-2 diesels were delivered to the B&M. Numbered 201–212, these engines truly ushered in the second generation of B&M power, close to a decade and a half after six GP18s were delivered in 1961. By year's end, 1977, 18 GP40-2s were delivered in the 300 series, completing the new power program. Once all 30 locomotives were on the property, crew runs, crew-change points, power-servicing locations, and work assignments were changed to take full advantage of the new power's capabilities. Whereas B&M power previously layed over at Rigby between assignments, the new "second generation policy" calls for crews to merely headpin from the arriving train for quick servicing, attach their power to a westbound train already made up, and, after the required tests, depart westbound. Contrary to their impression, the two shots on this page were taken "on the run"! (BALL)

Although they wear the colors of the Pinsly short line railroad family, high bells and long-hood-forward operation are clues to the NYC heritage of St. Johnsbury & Lamoille County's two GP9s. As they make up their train for St. Johnsbury in front of the Morrisville, Vt., depot in the summer of 1968 (left), who would have guessed that this rambling short line would struggle through state ownership, numerous abandonments, and three different names over the next decade! All of this was behind, and the future looked bright as an ex-D&H RS3 in the fresh colors of the Lamoille Valley Railway headed up the Morrisville–to–St. Johnsbury freight in late September 1978 (below) amid an early peak of autumn foliage.

At right, with her sharp exhaust echoing off surrounding hillsides, Steamtown's ex–Canadian Pacific G5 4-6-2 #1278 charges onto the steel trestle over the narrow but spectacularly deep Brockway Mills Gorge on a glorious September 1978 day. The Steamtown museum has running rights over the Green Mountain Railroad, operator of this former Rutland trackage above Bellows Falls, Vt. (BOYD, BOYD, BALL)

Autumn's beautiful stillness is interrupted by a car on Route 11 and the contented burbling of Springfield Terminal Railway's 44-ton GE locomotive #1 heading down from Springfield, Vt., along the Black River toward Charleston, N.H., and the interchange with Boston & Maine's Connecticut River Line. In another mile, the 44-tonner will tangle with car traffic across the joint rail-highway Cheshire Bridge over the Connecticut River into New Hampshire. No trouble should be encountered, however, since the little railroad owns the bridge and the toll-paying cars will have to wait their turn! The date is September 30, 1976.

A few miles downriver, we have Steamtown, foremost operator of large steam locomotives in New England. In addition to its own regular and special operations on the Green Mountain Railroad, the Steamtown Foundation made Nickel Plate Berkshire #759 available from its collection for the High Iron Company to overhaul and operate on a wide variety of trips ranging from Kansas City to Roanoke, and Binghamton, N.Y. On October 27–28, 1973, the much-traveled 2-8-4 made a run under Steamtown sponsorship from Boston via the B&M and CV to Montpelier, Vt. Following the route of the old *Alouette*, #759 steamed northward (above right) near Franklin, N.H., on B&M trackage.

The regular tourist operations of Steamtown take place between the museum site at Riverside, just north of Bellows Falls, Vt., and the depot at Chester, twelve scenic miles up the former Rutland trackage now operated by the Green Mountain Railroad. Chester is a picturesque little New England community (below left) in which the visiting steam trains seem right at home. The annual Steamtown Railfan's Weekend provides an opportunity to get all the museum's operable engines under steam as a spectacular event for the faithful. On October 30, 1976, three ex-CPR G5 4-6-2s are side by side under steam for a group night photo session in a scene reminiscent of any passenger engine terminal of the 1940s. (BALL, BALL, BOYD, BOYD)

Perhaps it's because of its fleeting charm that Indian summer's lovely bronze and gold season is tinged with melancholy this beautiful day. It is September 30, 1976, and the temperature in Claremont, N.H., is nearing 80 degrees. The coming of winter is certainly on no one's mind, that is, unless you are over by the Claremont & Concord Railway, watching the train arrive with winter's highway salt. #31, pictured at left, is indeed arriving with five cars of salt, heading toward the former B&M freight house, now C&C's general office. The 19-mile line comprises a segment of the former B&M Claremont branch, plus the former Claremont Railway. Out of the picture, just to the right, is C&C's piggyback ramp near the general office; what a sight it would be, seeing the trailers behind that little diesel!

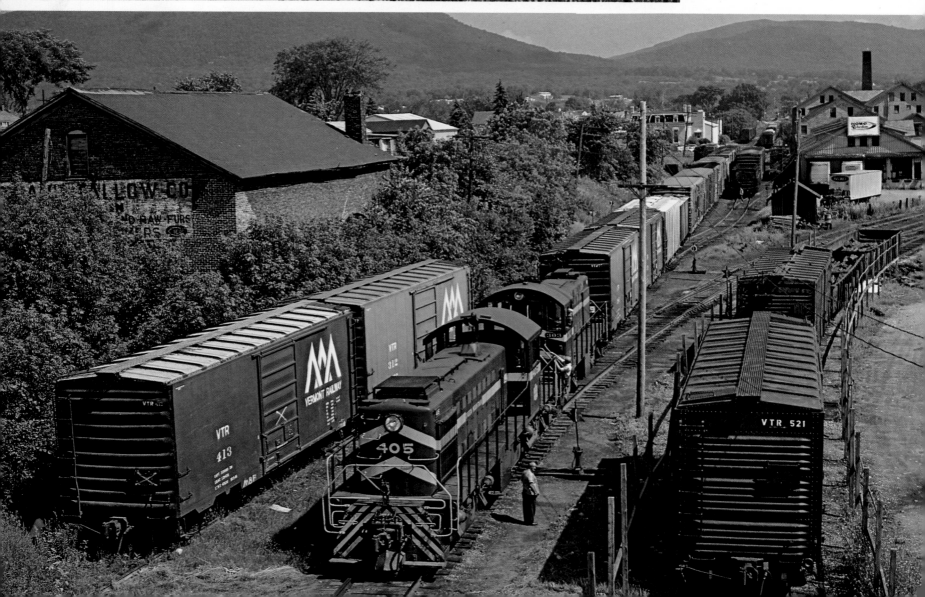

Old New England vividly recalls a vanished past...it has been said you need not try to imagine the Battle of Lexington, for you can see it! Perhaps this adage can be applied to the Rutland Railway, whose colorful history ended in 1962. Firmly anchored in its namesake community, the Rutland reached outward to the Canadian border, Lake Ontario, N.H., and even Albany, N.Y. But for all its mileage, the Rutland had minimal traffic, and a labor dispute prompted its abandonment in 1962. In an unprecedented move that would become the pattern for many other "resurrections" in the future, the state of Vermont purchased the viable segments of the old Rutland and appointed "designated operators" to run them. The Green Mountain Railroad took over the line from Rutland to Bellows Falls and adopted the Rutland's green and yellow colors as its own. At lower left, the last locomotive of Rutland heritage on the property, GMR RS1 #405, is seen working with ex-D&H S4 switcher #303 in downtown Rutland in July 1972.

The line from Burlington, Vt., south through Rutland to the B&M at North Bennington became the Vermont Railway which opted for a brilliant red-and-white version of the Rutland stripes. VTR RS3 #602—former Lehigh & Hudson River #3—is making good time with southbound symbol freight RC-2 below Wallingford (above) in July 1972 en route to North Bennington. (BALL, BOYD, BOYD)

Here is the quiet season again, a pause in Indian summer before the next act commences. Below right, Boston & Maine's Minute Man GP9 #1737 leads two mates and NE-87 up Shirley Hill in Lunenburg, Mass., on October 21, 1978; on the rear end, GP40-2 #300, "John W. Barriger", does the shoving. At immediate left, Boston & Maine's NW2 switcher #1202 heads the tool train out of East Deerfield, Mass., on October 1, 1978. That museum-piece diner is fresh out of the shop. Below, even a drizzle cannot dampen the luck of finding Central Vermont's only Geep in the original green and yellow, heading a black and red RS11 northward out of Bethel, Vt., on October 22, 1978. The unit was repainted in the old scheme after it was placed in test service to see how long a diesel could run between major overhauls. At upper right, B&M's Portland local is shown at Wakefield, Mass., in the spring of 1959. The picture is included both out of love for the maroon paint scheme and to show how badly passenger service had deteriorated by the decade of the '60s. (BALL, BOYD, DONAHUE, BALL)

During the 1970s a number of developments brought sweeping change to the railroad industry. Amtrak "standardized the passenger train," new short lines came into being, and municipal operating authorities entered the commuter business, to mention but a few. Along with terms like *abandonment, merger, takeover, consolidation,* and the like came new color—some of which is shown on these two pages.

Above, a "first generation" United Aircraft turbo train pulls into Providence on July 16, 1974, the magnificent Rhode Island capitol building for backdrop. At right, and bounding through the blazing foliage on the Southbridge branch just outside Webster, Mass., Providence & Worcester's U18B is a refreshing new sight in New England railroading. The P&W became a prosperous independent in 1973 after the bankrupt Penn Central stopped making lease payments to the P&W's owners.

The PC bankruptcy left the former NH and NYC commuter service in Boston a shambles, and the Massachusetts Bay Transportation Authority and Boston & Maine Railroad teamed up to revitalize the south-side operations. Until new locomotives could be delivered, MBTA leased the four Delaware & Hudson PA4 passenger units. At upper right, D&H 18 and 19 are passing each other just south of the Fort Point Channel drawbridges on November 16, 1977. At lower right, wearing the colors that would be applied to all new locomotives, Geep #7538 was the only one of her kind around Boston in November 1977. (*Turbo,* BALL: *all others,* BOYD)

Boiling out a "skyscape" that would have done a heavy I-4 New Haven Pacific proud, privately owned 2-8-0 #97, formerly of the Birmingham & Southeastern, rolls a passenger consist through Shelton, Conn., down from Waterbury toward Danbury in June 1968. Now a regular attraction at the Valley Railroad's museum in Essex, Conn., the 97 shared a night scene (left) on June 7, 1975 with another Alabama engine, former Sumter & Choctaw 2-6-2 103. The event was the Valley's annual Railfan Day.

Occasional visitors to New England have been the Canadian National's fan trip engines. 4-8-4 #6218 made it all the way to New London, Conn., in April 1967 over the Central Vermont, while successor 4-8-2 #6060 ventured into Portland, Me., on July 7, 1974. More typical of their runs, however, would be the 6218 rolling homeward into a golden afternoon out of Goderich, Ont., in October 1965 (right), or "Bullet-nosed Betty" 6060 hitting Jordan Bridge south of Hamilton, Ont., at 80 mph in August 1968 (top right) on one of its timetabled every-Saturday-and-Wednesday runs from Toronto to Niagara Falls. (97 top, DONAHUE; all others, BOYD)

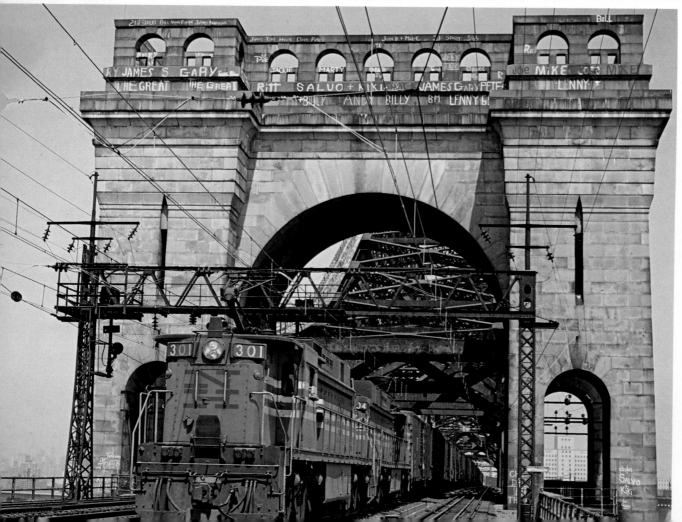

To the uninitiated, here is the grand McGinnis New Haven, with its bold, geometric "NH" scheme. To the seasoned New Haven railroader and fan alike: twilight, nay downfall, of a once magnificent railroad.

Above, the electrics are gone, but a still snazzy *Merchants Limited* cants to the curve past tower SS 44 at South Norwalk en route to Boston behind FL9s in August of '66. The line in the foreground is the Danbury branch. At upper right, in this April 1968 view, the standard equipment is gone and MUs "own the job" all the way between New Haven and New York. The westbound train is passing Peck tower (one T. J. Donahue's second home). At right, an EP5 "jet" speeds train No. 182 eastbound through Green's Farms, Conn., in June of '61, while, at left, a pair of ex-Virginian freight motors hum through Hell Gate's spans, heading symbol NG-3 into Bay Ridge yard on June 30, 1967. (DONAHUE, BALL, BALL, DONAHUE)

After the inclusion of New Haven into Penn Central (along the NH they called it a rape!) and the advent of Amtrak, changes started to happen—fast! There stood New Haven's great web of catenary, built to last forever, while under the wires Penn Central and Amtrak seemingly cluttered the rails with a little bit of everything, changing from day to day. At left, and on one of her first runs, Amtrak's platinum mist GG1 # 902 whips mail train 16's array of ex-NYC Flexi-Vans, caboose and bags eastbound across the Norwalk draw on June 15, 1972. At right, vintage ex-New Haven MUs—not only a rarity among Turbos and Gs, but east of Stamford—head through Noroton Heights, Conn., en route to New Haven on Labor Day 1972. At lower left, this is the *Yankee Clipper*! The Turbo train is pictured eastbound through Stamford, Conn., on April 25, 1970, while, below, on the same day, a trio of Alcos powers GB-2 eastward through Stamford. (BALL)

Today, on the New Haven. Yes, there are still locations that "look as always," but times are changing things. ATC and reverse traffic control are eliminating the semaphores, and soon commercial power (from Connecticut Light & Power's huge high-tension structures) will be used for the overhead. The E60, at left, is pictured westbound through Darien, Conn., with the customary train of "AmCans" on March 18, 1978. The antirock window protectors are known as "battle-zone screens" or "ghetto grilles." At lower left, a set of M2s slice through a blizzard, eastbound through Noroton Heights on February 12, 1978. The double signals displaying *advance approach* are approach boards to Stamford. At right, two Alco vignettes on the Long Island: FA control Cab #616 passing through Mill Neck, N.Y., en route to Oyster Bay in August 1977, and S2 switcher #443, rumbling through Sunnyside yard, Long Island City, on April 16, 1970. (*FA*, BOYD; *all others*, BALL)

I view these two pans with poignant feelings. Both the Turboliner (as it was initially called) and the EP-5 ignitron rectifier electric were dreams on drafting boards that when built and placed in service never lived up to their great expectations. Turbo had continuous nitty-gritty problems such as oil leaks and turbine shutdowns; the EP-5 jets had a rash of electrical fires. Both are pictured westbound through Byram, Conn., on June 18, 1970. (BALL)

2

CRISIS, CORRIDOR, CONFIDENCE

AMTRAK
CENTRAL RAILROAD CO. OF NEW JERSEY
CONSOLIDATED RAIL CORP. (CONRAIL)
DELAWARE AND HUDSON RAILWAY CO.
ERIE LACKAWANNA RAILWAY
LEHIGH AND HUDSON RIVER RAILWAY CO.
LEHIGH VALLEY RAILROAD CO.
METROPOLITAN TRANSPORTATION AUTHORITY
NEW JERSEY DEPARTMENT OF TRANSPORTATION
NEW YORK CENTRAL SYSTEM
NEW YORK, SUSQUEHANNA AND WESTERN RAILROAD CO.
PENN CENTRAL TRANSPORTATION CO.
READING COMPANY

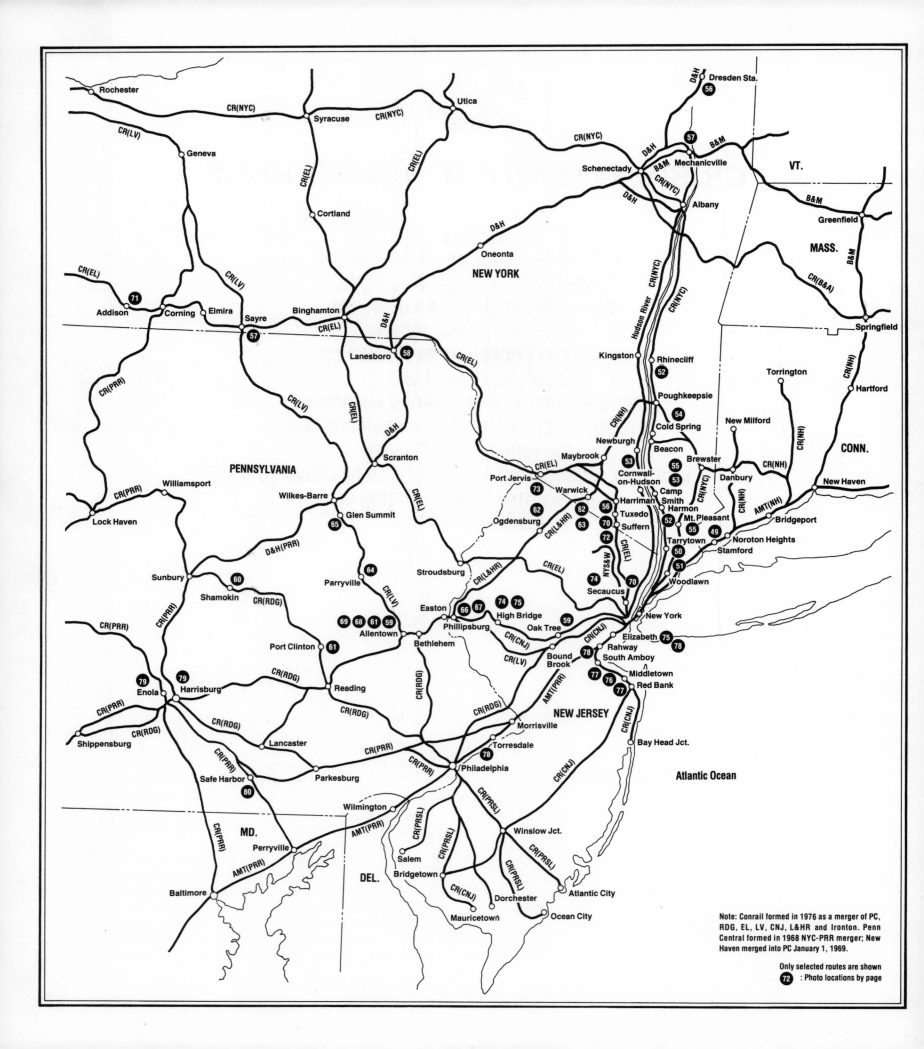

Rochester

CR(NYC) Syracuse CR(NYC) Utica

CR(LV) CR(NYC)

Geneva CR(EL) CR(EL)

D&H Dresden Sta.
56

Cortland 57 B&M

Schenectady B&M Mechanicville

D&H CR(NYC)

Albany VT.

NEW YORK B&M Greenfield

Oneonta MASS.

CR(EL) D&H

Addison 71 Corning Elmira Sayre Binghamton

CR(B&A)

CR(LV) CR(LV)

57 CR(EL) D&H

Lanesboro 58 CR(EL)

Springfield

Kingston Rhinecliff 52

CR(LV) Poughkeepsie Torrington

CR(EL) CR(LV) Scranton 54

PENNSYLVANIA CR(EL) Cold Spring New Milford CONN.

D&H Newburgh Beacon

Williamsport Wilkes-Barre Maybrook 53 Brewster Hartford

CR(PRR) Port Jervis Cornwall- Camp 55 Danbury CR(NH)

Glen Summit 73 Warwick on-Hudson 53 Smith New Haven

Lock Haven 65 62 62 56 Harriman Harmon 52 Mt. Pleasant AMT(NH)

CR(EL) Ogdensburg CR(L&HR) 63 70 Tuxedo Suffern 55 49 Bridgeport

D&H(PRR) 64 72 Tarrytown Noroton Heights

Sunbury 60 Parryville Stroudsburg CR(L&HR) CR(EL) 50 Stamford

Shamokin CR(RDG) CR(LV) 74 51 Woodlawn

CR(PRR) Easton CR(L&HR) 74 75 Secaucus 70

Port Clinton 69 68 61 59 66 67 High Bridge New York

CR(PRR) 61 Allentown Phillipsburg Oak Tree 59 CR(CNJ) Elizabeth 75 78

Bethlehem CR(CNJ) Rahway 78

79 CR(RDG) Reading CR(LV) Bound 78 South Amboy

Enola 79 Harrisburg Brook 77 Middletown

Shippensburg CR(PRR) CR(RDG) 77 76 Red Bank 77

CR(PRR) Lancaster CR(PRR) Morrisville NEW JERSEY CR(CNJ)

CR(RDG) Torresdale Bay Head Jct.

Safe Harbor Parkesburg 78 Atlantic Ocean

80 CR(PRR) Philadelphia

Wilmington CR(PRSL)

MD. CR(PRR) AMT(PRR) Winslow Jct.

Perryville DEL. Salem CR(PRSL) CR(PRSL)

Bridgetown CR(PRSL)

Baltimore AMT(PRR) CR(CNJ) Atlantic City

Dorchester

Mauricetown Ocean City

Note: Conrail formed in 1976 as a merger of PC,
RDG, EL, LV, CNJ, L&HR and Ironton. Penn
Central formed in 1968 NYC-PRR merger; New
Haven merged into PC January 1, 1969.

Only selected routes are shown
72 : Photo locations by page

I N MY Johnny-come-lately love affair with second-generation diesels and railroading, I've always singled out the Lehigh Valley as my eastern favorite. Geography, Alcos, and company pride, I'm sure, come to bear in my selection of the Valley. Perhaps, too, the tinge of frustration and identification I get when I see someone or something *really trying* to succeed—feeling it should win when, for unforeseeable reasons, it can't—has a deep effect on my allegiance or attachment. To me, the Valley represented the best in Northeastern freight railroading into the 1970s. Notwithstanding, I'd like to turn to an earlier Lehigh Valley, the "pre–second-generation Lehigh Valley" of 1960, to point out what I feel was the nitty-gritty realization that America's *passenger* trains could not survive as part-and-parcel private-sector business.

By 1960, the Lehigh Valley had discontinued six of its 10 mainline passenger trains and was fighting to drop the east- and westbound *John Wilkes* and *Maple Leaf.* As early as December 1958, the road had been fighting to chop all passenger runs. By 1961, when the railroad finally succeeded in dropping the last two trains, the Valley became the 17th railroad in the United States to cease passenger-train operation since 1945. The Lehigh Valley was the first *major* trunk line to take this drastic step. In early 1961, Lehigh Valley's president C. A. Major warned: "Our closing [of passenger service] will create a public awareness of what is happening to the railroads in this country. The powers that be must make up their minds if the U.S. is to have a first-class railroad system. If they don't provide financial aid one way or another, railroads will continue to fade from the American scene." The story is a familiar one; the Valley's passenger service began to dry up when the Pennsylvania Turnpike, crossing northern Pennsylvania, was opened in 1946, rendering its death blow. In 1945, the railroad carried over 2 million passengers; five years later, 1 million; by 1959, 420,000. The 1960 total was 250,000.

The plight of our nation's rail passenger service was, in my opinion, never so dramatically brought home than when the New York Central announced on July 26, 1966, that it was ending all through passenger train service effective January 1, 1967. I have saved the clipping from the front page of the July 26 *Wall Street Journal,* its headlines stating: "The New York Central's proposed cancellation of long distance passenger service would mean the end of the *20th Century Limited.*" Reading on, the article states that the railroad would "institute high speed shuttle service between 80 paired cities, with runs all under 200 miles." The article continued, quoting Wayne Hoffman, executive vice-president of the line: "The railroad will eliminate overnight sleepers, dining cars and other luxuries." Finally, the *Journal* mentioned that "The New York Central and the Pennsylvania R. R. are working out final phases leading to a merger of the two carriers."

I'd like to once again go back to 1960 and take a personal look at the New York Central. For starters, I began commuting that year on the Central out of Hartsdale, N.Y., to my job at ACF. *Somehow,* the Central got wind of the fact that I was a newcomer to their rails and, lo and behold, a "Welcome Newest Commuter! Commuting Tip Kit" (as they called it) arrived in the mail. The handy kit contained a booklet entitled "How to Get and Hold the Right Job," a brochure on the Social Security card—"What it is, What you do with it &

Why"—an application for an SS number, and complete maps of New York City, the subways, and elevated lines. The kit also contained the "How to Recognize and Deal with the Old Commuter or Commuter-Watcher's Manual," a pamphlet, "Your Commuter Tips," the current timetables, and a set of the Fogg P&LE/NYC post cards, omitting the steam, of course. Honestly! I have saved this little kit and am still indebted to the New York Central and its sharp PR Department for it.

As for the job, it, too, brought me in contact with the New York Central. I cut my teeth, you could say, on the new ACF 25-lb. P.S.I. Flexi-Flow car for Central's bulk cement-to-truck service. I was aware of the fact that the Central was the nation's leading transporter of new automobiles and in 1960 was operating the fastest scheduled freight in the world. I was equally aware of New York Central's pace-setting Marketing Department for the development of new services, equipment, and prices. From atomic switchlamps to air flotation devices to protect the shipping of missiles, Central was the embodiment of *"The Road to the Future."* It was a research-oriented railroad that was convinced its total management team was second to none in the industry. At the company's headquarters over at "466 Lex," it was stressed that "Railroading is a lifelong learning process." Central was real estate—big real estate. It was the leader in push-button yards and applied research—maintaining research labs for new approaches, "not just refinements," as they liked to say. Central was CTC, streamlined M of W operations, microwave communications, and a railroad obsessed with diversification and mergers. In 1960, Central studied a merger with the Baltimore & Ohio, with hopes for a later tie with the C&O. Though it never happened, I still think this merger would have been the right one.

Nineteen sixty and the next three years brought quite a bit of business travel into my life. Here, too, the New York Central played a part. My being in the railroad-supply business meant plenty of trips to Chicago. On many an afternoon I'd walk over to GCT, pick up my already-made-out tickets from Central's Commercial Accounts window, and head for track 26 and the *20th Century Limited*. Anyone who has ever visited Grand Central Terminal will remember the big train departure board and its electronic flip signs. Watching one was like watching a score board, as train names and destinations flipped past until the designated sign was reached. *The Knickerbocker; New England States; Ohio State Limited; 20th Century Limited; The Wolverine; Lake Shore Limited; Southwestern Limited* . . . and on and on.

The familiar red and gray roll sign for the *Century* beckons its riders to the check-in counter and the walk down the red carpet to the beautiful train. In a few moments the hubbub of Grand Central is behind us as we're helped aboard this elegant traveling home by a smiling, white-jacketed porter. A "Welcome Aboard" folder has been placed in each room, describing the *Century*'s services, including valet and room service, availability of an Underwood typewriter, electric shaver, and shoe shine. The mid-train lounge and the observation Lookout Lounge are both described in the folder, as is the diner—rather, the Century Room—and all of the trimmings. "Booaard." A gentle pull and we're off for Chicago!

Immediately, fantasies take over. I am a child—excited and filled with wanderlust! There *is* magic about the *20th Century Limited*. Once more, I am aboard her for the next 16 hours. I walk through her cars, down the quiet, narrow aisles, until I reach the observation car. Sure, I ride these same rails every day on my commuter train, but this is different. I am aboard the *20th Century Limited*! Our observation car is warm and cheery in its light beiges and tans. The lamps are aglow, ceiling lights subdued, and fresh-cut flowers add the perfect touch. Unlike my commuter train, the *Century* glides. The click-click clack-clack is not to be heard, just a pleasant muffled rumble. Complimentary hors d'oeuvres, a Scotch, and the most beautiful view of the Hudson ever seen by man. All of this before dinner! Quietly, I try to take in all of this wonderment, and I know that I am not alone in my thoughts. Surely, there is no one on board tonight who is not 10 years old in his heart.

That was the *early* '60s, and change was in the air. For those of us watching the railroads, our heads were spinning with passenger-train discontinuances, mergers, paint schemes, new diesels. *Second generation* is a term we use for the new high-horsepower hood-unit diesels that were coming to the railroads; I submit that *second-generation railroading* is really what we are talking about. In 1960, as I said, Central was eyeing B&O and, possibly, C&O. In less than two years, on January 12, 1962, to be exact, the agreement for the merger of the New York Central and its historic rival Pennsylvania was approved by the board of directors of both companies. In 1961, Central sought approximately 50 percent control of the B&O through an exchange offer, looking toward a C&O/NYC/B&O merger. At the same time, the C&O was seeking exclusive control of the B&O. In the meantime, the Norfolk and Western had applied for approval of a merger with the Nickel Plate, the leasing and ultimate stock control of the Wabash, and the purchase from the Pennsy of its important Sandusky Branch. Central requested to be included in this emerging N&W system. For a while it looked like 1961 would bring on a new, giant Norfolk and Western/Pennsylvania Railroad system and the Central did some behind-the-boardroom-door scrambling to be included in the C&O!

I've been using 1960 as an obvious bench-mark year in railroading and would like to return again to this time of change. On July 20, 1960, an oral argument proposing a merger between the Erie Railroad and Lackawanna Railroad was held before the full Interstate Commerce Commission in Washington. This presentation was the culmination of four years of study that commenced in April 1956 to look at a consolidation of the Erie and the Lackawanna (and Delaware & Hudson). It was pointed out at the hearing that coordination between the two railroads was already in effect or planned, and the close geographic relationship of the two companies indicated definite opportunities for improvements in service along with great economies. Getting into well-spelled-out specifics, the principals revealed that joining the two railroads would offer many opportunities to reduce costs by combining duplicate facilities and operations—more than $13 million annually. On September 15, 1960, the merger of the Erie and Lackawanna was approved by an ICC order setting October 15, 1960, as the effective date.

In a merger there are always "casualties" such as the total dominance of one former company over another or complete loss of historic presence, visual identification, morale, or what have you. The E-L merger, in my book, was a classic exception. The management drew the best from the former roads, and, appropriately, the passenger paint scheme remained very much Lackawanna while the freight scheme was very much Erie. Somehow, the new railroad could not bury the past of the two predecessor roads. The second generation came to the E-L in May 1963 with the delivery of 15 new Alco Century 424 locomotives, replacing 36 older first-generation units. Along the way, the hyphen was dropped between Erie and Lackawanna, but the past "remained in effect" with each road's unique paint schemes and equipment intermingled. In 1964, the road settled on a "new" paint scheme, based on the former Lackawanna maroon, gray, and yellow that soon became a favorite for railfans.

Maybe, for geographic reasons, the two railroads *couldn't* be separated. I do not know. They ran parallel across New York State's southern tier between Binghamton and Corning, and both roads served the Buffalo Gateway. Erie Lackawanna seemed a natural. Back in August 1959, before the merger, the

Lackawanna started using Erie's tracks between Binghamton and Corning in order to eliminate duplicate trackage. Surely, both roads knew the combination was necessary in order to survive.

The new railroad became "The Friendly Service Route" and lived up to its slogan. I never rode on a long-haul EL passenger train, so I cannot speak about the service (although comments I've heard were usually very favorable); I *have* ridden several MU commuter trains out of Hoboken, however, and would like to share some observations. The equipment, first of all, is ancient, but it works. Close to 40,000 people depend on the EL commuter trains each day. Sure, riders throw facetious remarks at the equipment, but never at the O.T. performance. "We've got air-conditioning, folks, as long as the windows don't stick," I heard a conductor say on a warm, muggy night. "You can see the dents where the arrowheads hit," mused a commuter. A man comfortably propped in the wicker seat of the club car said he "expected to see Harold Lloyd in the motorman's cab." No matter, summer, fall, winter, spring, the railroad works. When there is a heavy snowfall, the Erie Lackawanna runs equipment up and down all its lines throughout the night to make damn sure the railroad will be clear for the morning rush. Every morning, I listen to the traffic delays broadcast over WCBS radio and only once did I hear the EL was running late—and that was because there was a warehouse fire and firemen had laid hoses across the track! The PC and Long Island, on the other hand, made the WCBS reports day in and day out (except weekends). Wasn't it Thomas Jefferson who said: "Agriculture, manufacture, commerce, and navigation, the four pillars of our prosperity, are the most thriving when left to individual enterprise." Sic Transit Gloria. . . .

As I stated earlier, the merger of the Pennsylvania and New York Central into Penn Central took place on February 1, 1968. In just a little over two years, on June 21, 1970, to be exact, Penn Central formally came apart at the seams when Paul A. Gorman, then authorized chairman of the board, filed a petition of bankruptcy in the federal district court in Philadelphia. Incredibly, the greatest and most powerful transportation system and one of the five top businesses in the country had gone under. The *New York Times* called the PC bankruptcy "the most monumental failure in the nation's history." On paper, the figures were grim—current liabilities, including debt due within a year, of $749 million, with only $7.3 million of cash to meet a semi-monthly payroll of $26 million. For many of us, a bad dream from the beginning, had ended—or sort of ended.

For the next several years, I felt I was watching a giant die a slow, agonizing death. Inadequate maintenance resulted in slow orders of 6 to 10 miles an hour on well over 9,000 miles of track, and it was not unusual to see two and even three crews get outlawed, handling a train that a couple of years earlier was easily handled by one crew. Trains were often held up on slow orders for such long periods of time they would frequently arrive at a destination and find the newly assigned engines gone. As equipment was delayed, equipment ownership costs and payments for rented equipment rose; the sickness got worse. On June 20, 1975, PC's president Jervis Langdon said it all: "We are incurably deficit. To deal with the situation, it [Penn Central] has to be subsidized."

Getting into the scenario that led to Conrail would be both amusing and frustrating—certainly too much for this book. I was doing some work for the FRA, and was closely in touch with the P&W, L&HR, and PC at the time. I was a staunch member of Bruce Sterzing's (D&H) "All-Volunteer Northeast Rail Brand X Marching and Chowder Society"—a small, informal, but elite group (as Bruce put it). In 1975, I was also trying to spearhead a privately owned captive container train over the CP-D&H-PC that, for a while, looked like it was going to go (I cannot say get off the ground!). In the interim, I was privy to an initial meeting at Six Penn Center in which the first *brown* CR paint scheme was unveiled. To this day, I still do not know why "Premier Blue" was settled on.

Conrail . . . sounds like "against rail"; the logo looks like a snail. As I write this, CR looks more and more like a blue Penn Central. Lord knows, I want railroads to survive, but in the private sector. I sometimes feel this country is in an antibusiness surge in which every corporate mistake or imperfection, from a defective can of dog food to a single malfunction of a gidget-gadget, becomes an excuse for slowing technological development, proposing new economic controls, and urging nationalization of private enterprise. I believe, however, that it is not too late to rekindle the fire of private initiative and really reindustrialize America. I hope to see America once again proud, self-sustaining, able to defend itself, if need be, and able to maintain a high standard of living. No, news from Conrail is not good . . . shades of the Penn Central nightmare; continued need for a steady infusion of money from Washington; warnings to commercial lenders that the latest plan for reaching profitability rests on "optimistic" assumptions that might not be met, etc., etc. And, in the words of the 1979 USRA report to Congress, "Even if all business plan projections are exceeded, Conrail's ability to become financially self-sustaining by 1983 is not assured." It just sounds too familiar.

SNAFU! Waiting by today's trackside, hoping for something "new or different" to come by can often be a thankless task. In a world of E60s and M2s, a sight such as this gladdens the heart of the photographer and makes almost any wait worthwhile! Upon hearing that the 1909-vintage semaphore signals were going to quickly fall victim to the new signaling system being installed, I decided to document the usual E60 under the ancient Ives tinplate-looking signal bridge not too far from my house. After an hour's wait, the undeni-able sound of fast-approaching Alco diesels was heard, and what was coming was anybody's guess. Sad to see it was a G that was stricken, but the two black RS3s raising hell to keep Amtrak's schedule respectable made the wait well worth it! (Wasn't it Alco who advertised their RS3 with the slogan "To meet the changing motive power needs of America's railroads"?) In case anyone cares, the train is westbound No. 143, *The Betsy Ross*. The date: January 14, 1979. (BALL)

Casualties of Penn Central were heavy, and there was always that frustrating desire to turn your back on the "worms" and forget they even existed. Yet there was also that nagging curiosity to go back to the tracks and look for survivors from better days. Unlike cast-in-the-mold diesels, which looked alike in black, the paint couldn't hide the distinct railroad personalities of electric locomotives. Such was the case for the brief appearance of ex-NYC and ex-New Haven electrics in PC black. Below, that snazzy train with the Santa Fe bag is Empire Service train No. 71 en route to Buffalo and its Toronto connection. At immediate right, the fireman enjoys the river air at the helm of No. 70, heading toward GCT. Both trains are pictured at Tarrytown, N.Y. on July 3, 1973. At far right, the pans are locked down on EP-5 #4977, coasting at speed onto third-rail territory at Woodlawn, N.Y., on November 17, 1970. The train is No. 1369 from New Haven. (BALL)

The evolution of New York Central's final years is pictured on this spread, wrapped up by a post-NYC, post-PC hospital train, pictured at lower right, heading west along the Hudson River at Camp Smith, N.Y., on May 16, 1978. If you look carefully, you'll see that the decrepit-looking FL9s in the hospital train are now carrying three-digit 480-series numbers in lieu of their normal 5000 series numbers; both units, #484 and #488, are heading west—way west—to Morrison-Knudsen at Boise, Idaho, for rebuilding into Amtrak units with head-end electrical power (HEP). It is presumed the other dead diesels are en route to the DeWitt shops in Syracuse for major rebuilding.

At upper left, and in slightly better days, the elegance of New York Central, though covered with road grime, is still evident in the Alco and EMD units laying over at Harmon, N.Y., in September 1962 awaiting their Chicago trains. Below, the *Ohio State Limited* and the *20th Century Limited* are but memory as an E8 in the simplified "cigar-band" paint scheme leaves Rhinecliff, N.Y., with Empire Service for Albany and Syracuse in April 1968. At right, a Central coal train thunders past the old O&W interchange at Cornwall-on-Hudson, N.Y., in April 1968 behind a striking first-generation diesel lashup. (BALL, DONAHUE, DONAHUE, BALL)

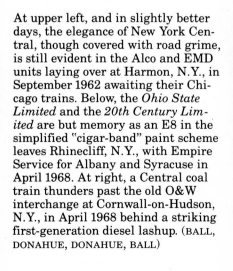

There are days in our lives that we will never forget. May 16, 1978, was one of those days for me. It was a day spent along the broad reach of the Hudson and along the old tracks of the New York Central. The wind stirred the moist, wooded air and created bobbing, silvery whitecaps out on the water. The buds were greening in the hills, and I could sense the threat of their bursting into full leaves overnight. Puffy, white clouds blew across the crystal sky, dancing like playful lambs. This was one of those days when you are glad you're alive!

Alone, along the Hudson, whose muscles are still bulging with winter's meltwater; alone in some of the most magnificent river country in the world. Solitude is what you call it, and I firmly believe that there are mysteries and glories in the world that will never be revealed to you if you never leave the multitude. I also believe that solitude doesn't take you away from people; rather, it draws you closer. "Go cherish your soul," said Ralph Waldo Emerson; Henry David Thoreau exclaimed, "I never found the companion that was companionable as solitude." I continuously thank God for the off-the-highway America that train photography has taken me to!

"Steelton 1952" it said on the rails, and I realized I was standing next to a right-of-way that was last upgraded when the mighty Hudson, Mohawks and Niagaras pounded past with the Great Steel Fleet. Surrounded by this historic land, the realization of the fragile impermanence of even a mighty New York Central suddenly struck me in the context of this short lifetime of changing history. And before me, a silent, white intruder, conceived in France and constructed in California, called Turbo and named *The Henry Hudson* clicked along the tracks toward Albany.

At right, and in the solitude of Valhalla, N.Y., a former New Haven FL9 greets the sunrise with Harlem Division train No. 938 from Brewster to New York City on November 1, 1979. At lower right, and back on the Hudson the following day, May 17, the Budd car from Poughkeepsie trundles through Camp Smith, N.Y., en route to Croton-Harmon and its New York City connection. (BALL)

Blessed with one of the sharpest paint schemes in the region and an acknowledged railfan for a chief executive, the Delaware & Hudson remained the bright spot in Northeastern railroading during the dark days of the collapse of its neighbors into Conrail. The favorites of the D&H freight locomotives were the elegant Alco Century 628s like the 613 (upper left) in pool service on the Erie Lackawanna in February 1972 as it charged through the accumulated snow on the passenger line at Harriman, N.Y., like a navy destroyer at flank speed through a North Sea swell. Sister units were in a more sedate setting (lower right) in October 1967 as they idled in the Mechanicville, N.Y., engine terminal beside a set of EMD SD45 demonstrators that the D&H would shortly purchase. D&H president Carl B. "Bruce" Sterzing got back the four ex–Santa Fe Alco PA passenger diesels that had been traded to General Electric and arranged with Amtrak and the state of New York to return passenger service to the Albany-Montreal route. In March 1975 PA4 #17 (lower left) zips the southbound *Adirondack* by Steele's General Store at Dresden Station, N.Y. Sterzing also acquired the nation's last pair of Baldwin RF16 "Sharks" and put them into freight service. It was the railfan social event of the season when the Sharks went to work on the "Owego Connection" between Binghamton, N.Y., and Sayre, Pa. Above, the pair enters Sayre on a beautiful July 23, 1975. (*Left page,* BOYD; *right page,* BALL)

The days are lengthening. The sun is returning. The whole year is beginning. The last ice has dropped from the branches, now free to sway in the breeze. It's after the winter solstice now, and it's all downhill from here. Each day is longer. Gradually, the season will fade into memories of the gentleness of snow and the joys of being out of doors. Spring cannot be too far away.

The railroad that *continued* to endear itself to me was the Lehigh Valley. Long after PAs and FAs and Cornell Red passenger trains, the Valley remained a favorite. Perhaps it was the Alcos or the paint. Whatever, the Valley seemed to

outclass its Eastern rivals from all standpoints of operations, but somehow couldn't hold on. I deeply regretted seeing the Valley go, more than any other pre-Conrail road. I know my feelings are shared.

The Lehigh Valley is pictured on this spread, as I like to remember it. The picture above of NE-84 passing beneath Starrucca Viaduct late on a March 1976 afternoon is, perhaps, my favorite in this book. NE-84's ultimate destination is Rigby Yard in Portland, Me., and D&H-LV pooled their power on the Allentown-Mechanicville segment of the run. (BOYD)

On this page, Indian summer! And change is in the air, borne on the first gusts of north wind. The cool, dry days of autumn are invigorating; the sky, a shimmering blue. Only the oak leaves resist the coming of winter, stubbornly holding on. Three Alco C420s penetrate the scene, at left, rushing eastbound BJ-2 through, appropriately, Oak Tree, N.J., on October 20, 1973. Below, the lead unit of a quartet of Alco Century 628s heads eastbound LV-2 into Allentown, Pa., on October 8, 1974. (BALL)

Generally regarded as one of the classiest color schemes in the entire Northeast, the Reading Company's elegant black and green "covered wagon" colors vanished in the early 1960s when all of its Fs and FAs were traded in on new GP30s, GP35s and C424s—except for three FP7s. Passenger units 900, 902, and 903 were kept on hand for a weekday push-pull Reading-Philadelphia commuter train, which utilized one unit on either end of a matched consist of traditional open-window coaches (the "third" unit was rotated as a spare). However, on May 6, 1973, the Reading ran an excursion for the National Railway Historical Society 60 from Reading to Shamokin, Pa., with the 900 and 902 back-to-back and pulling the coaches creating a vivid image of

the old *King Coal* as it departed Shamokin, above, in the early afternoon. Shamokin is in the heart of the anthracite coal region, and earlier that same day fans following the passenger special were treated to another image of the area as three grimy green Alco RS3s rumbled under the bridge, right, at Port Clinton with a heavily laden coal train out of West Cressona. The more common image of the "new" Reading is that of a hulking Alco Century 630 and a pair of smaller EMDs in March 1974 getting Philadelphia-bound freight AP-12, at right, rolling past R Tower at the west end of Allentown Yard. As soon as the Reading train clears the junction, that pair of Lehigh Valley Alcos will depart northward with its train for Lehighton. (BOYD)

One of the casualties of Conrail was the picturesque Lehigh & Hudson River Railway, operating as a bridge route around New York City. Survival is a harsh word to use, but L&HR's survival as a "black-ink carrier" depended on the Maybrook, N.Y., connection with the former New Haven and the direct Poughkeepsie Bridge gateway over the Hudson River into southern New England. On May 14, 1974, the Poughkeepsie Bridge was mysteriously destroyed by fire, and for L&HR the vital umbilical cord was cut. Then followed two years of struggling to survive only on local traffic and a gerrymandered interchange arrangement with Penn Central at Phillipsburg.

For obvious reasons, the road was a favorite among railfans—what with Alco diesels, back-country scenery and friendly employees. At upper left, two Century 420s creep down the former Susquehanna Hanford branch with cars for the New Jersey Zinc mine at Ogdensburg on a beautiful October 23, 1972. At lower left, #29 hiccups (the camera wasn't cocked), then belches (the camera *was* cocked), getting the Ogdensburg job westbound out of Warwick on March 11, 1973. In truth, the Alco's free-running turbocharger, not geared to the engine, suddenly speeds up to catch up with the engine's increased rpms, not supplying enough air in the meantime to obtain clean combustion. This results in Alco's endearing smoke! At right, we see two views of Alco's first Century 420 heading NE-3 past Baird's Lane, above, and through a 300mm telephoto lens heading toward us and the Warwick yard. The scenes were taken in October 1977 and April 1975, respectively. (*Left page*, BALL; *right page*, BOYD)

On April 1, 1976, on the day of—and as a condition of—the Conrail merger, the little Delaware & Hudson almost doubled its route mileage by picking up trackage rights over Conrail lines to such remote points as Buffalo, N.Y., Newark, N.J., Harrisburg and Philadelphia, Pa., and Potomac Yard in Alexandria, Va.! To provide motive power for the expanded service, the government permitted the D&H a pick of motive power from the pre-Conrail lines, and instead of the "junk" everyone had expected they'd get stuck with, the D&H acquired some prime new power in the form of the Lehigh Valley and Reading's newest EMD locomotives. From the Lehigh Valley came GP38-2s and Alco C420s, while from the Reading came GP39-2s to match identical brand-new units just being delivered to the D&H at the time (in keeping with the Bicentennial spirit of 1976, the D&H GP39-2s were given the 7600 number series). Although D&H power had been a common sight in the valley of the Lehigh River above Allentown on a D&H/LV/Reading pool agreement, D&H symbol freight AM-1 from Allentown to Mechanicville is barely a month old as hastily relettered

former LV GP38-2 #7318 leads a mix of D&H and former Reading power through Parryville, Pa., above, just below Lehighton in May 1976.

In April 1972, Penobscot Mountain has not yet shaken off winter's barren chill, above right, as Lehigh Valley freight LV-2 drops down from Solomon's Gap and Glen Summit on the old CNJ main line overlooking the Nescopeck Valley. One of the LV's last gray and yellow Alco C420s leads a pair of borrowed Lehigh & Hudson River C420s in an interesting and unusual combination of locomotives. It's the other end of the season six years later as D&H freight AM-1 fights upgrade at the same location, right, on October 28, 1978. Still wearing its Reading green but with "temporary" D&H lettering, GP39-2 #7408 is leading a former-LV GP38-2 and a repainted D&H ex-LV C420 on the head end of the train with another LV/Reading Geep pair shoving hard on the rear. The rust-colored leaves are lingering in the setting sun of not just the day, but of the entire season, for it will take only one night of north wind to clear the trees and return the landscape to winter's stark nakedness. (BOYD)

The Delaware River is laced by three railroad bridges just below its confluence with the Lehigh River between the twin cities of Easton, Pa., and Phillipsburg, N.J. With Easton's skyline in the background, Delaware & Hudson's hot Chicago-to-Newark piggybacker *Apollo-2* is in the care of three new GP39-2s as it crosses Conrail's former Lehigh Valley bridge and enters New Jersey on December 5, 1976. Beneath the lead unit are the tracks of the old Pennsylvania R.R. "Bel-Del" line, which followed the east bank of the Delaware from Trenton nearly to the Delaware Water Gap; major pieces of the line, however, are now abandoned.

The "middle" of the three bridges carries the double-track main line of the Central Railroad of New Jersey—better known simply as the "Jersey Central." In August 1966, above right, a one-year-old SD35 is teamed up with a hulking Fairbanks-Morse Train Master on an eastbound

morning freight from Allentown, Pa., to Elizabeth, N.J. The top semaphore blade on the signal is just dropping down from its vertical "clear" indication as the train enters the Phillipsburg interlocking plant. That same semaphore is dropping again five years later, below right, for a Lehigh & Hudson River Alco C420 making a transfer delivery to the Jersey Central's Phillipsburg Yard on August 8, 1971. The lacy truss bridge, the northernmost of the three, belonged to the L&HR, but like the other two is now the property of Conrail. Prior to the Conrail merger Phillipsburg was served by no less than five bankrupt railroads: Lehigh Valley, Jersey Central, Lehigh & Hudson River, Erie Lackawanna, and Penn Central. It is now served by one railroad, Conrail, and sees Delaware & Hudson trains running on Conrail trackage rights. (BOYD, BOYD, BALL)

66

Allentown Yard has long been the melting pot of the anthracite region. Built originally by the Jersey Central, it played host to the Reading and Lehigh & Hudson River in the 1960s, but by the time Conrail arrived in 1976, the huge facility had witnessed an almost total change of occupants. The L&HR was the first to leave, withdrawing to little Hudson Yard above Phillipsburg, N.J., in November 1971, and the Jersey Central itself pulled out in April 1972, leaving the yard in the care of the Lehigh Valley, previously only an occasional visitor there with its main line passing by on the opposite side of the Lehigh River. Only the Reading remained essentially unchanged. Of course, the whole thing became Conrail on April 1, 1976.

One of the first units to be repainted in Conrail's "dress blues," SD35 #6024 was a frequent target of railfans' cameras in late 1976. It's leading a set of Penn Central blacks departing track 7 in "the Park" of the "Heavy Side" of Allentown Yard westbound for Buffalo, above, on December 19, 1976. Yet to be touched by Conrail's painters, Reading GP35 #3651, left, is being eased onto the turntable at Allentown in October 1976.

The west end of Allentown Yard is controlled by "R" Tower, a cozy wooden structure housing a modern interlocking plant. As a Lehigh Valley RS3 calmly burbles away, a section gang is busy replacing ties in an important switch at the throat of the yard as a westbound Reading job waits patiently, peering out from behind the distant trees. Step lively, guys; we can't keep the manifests waiting. (BOYD, BALL, BALL)

By adopting the passenger colors of the old Lackawanna at the time of its merger, the Erie Lackawanna emerged with one of the most richly handsome liveries in the Northeast. Opting for some of the biggest locomotives then available, the EL acquired no less than three variations of EMD's massive 20-cylinder 3600-horsepower SD45s; a pair of the "stretched" versions, special boilerless passenger SDP45s, are pulling an eastbound freight into Suffern, N.Y., top left, in November 1972. Another SDP45 is teamed up with an E8 on an eastbound freight along the beautiful Canisteo River in upstate New York in October 1974, above—there's nothing like autumn foliage and sunshine to bring out the best in a railroad.

The late afternoon sun on April 17, 1971, reflects upon an EL commuter train, middle left, crossing the Hackensack River drawbridge at the west end of Croxton Yard in Secaucus, N.J. The old Erie RS3 and veteran Stillwell coaches are living on borrowed time, though, for blue-and-silver state-owned U34CHs and streamlined push-pull cars are already taking over most of the EL commuter runs. The last trains to succumb to the push-pull equipment were the Hoboken–Port Jervis trains, because a dispute over the purchase of the new locomotives and cars between the states of New Jersey and New York kept E8s and a fleet of Stillwells running until September 1974. The southbound Saturday morning train No. 70 from Port Jervis, bottom left, rolls past the waterfall at Tuxedo, N.Y., in March 1973 with a matched set of two-tone Erie green Stillwells. (BALL, BALL, BOYD, DONAHUE)

November so often begins with low clouds that stretch on forever, offering only an occasional pillar of sunlight to fall to the ground. It grows dark at midday; a snowflake zigzags down, followed by another. Every now and then, a patch of blue sky opens up soon to be closed out by the dark clouds. Some more stray flakes looking for the ground, some more blue patches of sky. November is a teaser, warning of the bleak and overcast days that follow.

November 12, 1972, was just such a day. The morning sky was full of promise, full of sunshine. By noon, and by the time I had driven west to look for an Erie Lackawanna freight, whimsical November had all but dashed hopes for light. I parked the car, got up on the bridge, and as so often happens in November, the light readings fluctuated between f4 and 1.9 at ½50th of a second. Nearby, squirrels were scurrying, stockpiling their hoards before snow blankets the food supply.

The throb of EMD power resounds in the close by hills. Through the spans march two SDP45s, elephant style, with *Santa Fe-100*'s general merchandise in tow. The light—what little light there is—is splotchy as the freight rumbles past. What little light there was, I got, as seen at left. The trophy I got was, to me, well worth the drive, time, and cold ears!

On this page, a little fun. At upper right, no shootout at the OK Corral, but this is Erie Lackawanna? Proof that diesels have no prejudices comes with this shot of NE-74 heading into Port Jervis, N.Y., behind a pair of Burlington Northern SD45s on August 14, 1971. With the standardization of diesels, the pooling of run-through power has become one of the most prevalent changes in second-generation railroading. At lower right, two GE U34CH Jersey DOT commuter engines are caught just out of Port Jervis cavorting in a rare spree of freight service headed east through Rundel's Curve in July 1972. (BALL, BALL, BOYD)

It goes against my grain to write an "it's hard to believe" caption for every spread on northeast railroading, but here again I look at these once commonplace railroads and operations and have to think twice before I realize they're gone! Above, Susquehanna's transfer run from Little Ferry, N.J., to Croxton Yard is pictured at Secaucus, behind one of the snappy low-nosed GP18s on February 22, 1977. This job has now been discontinued, and as of New Year's 1978 the trustees of the Susquehanna had decided to try and liquidate the property. At left, a pair of Baldwin DR4-4-1500 "baby-face" diesels burble out of High Bridge, N.J., headed for Green Pond Junction and a connection with the Susquehanna with goods out of Allentown in September 1966. At upper right—and, baby, it's cold outside—during a lull in the onslaught of electric passenger trains, a Rudolph-red GP7 leads a GP40P under the Pennsy wires past Elmora Tower at Elizabeth, heading a Jersey Central shore train. The date is February 2, 1977. At lower right, ES-99's EL and CNJ power is seen at High Bridge on March 20, 1973. The unusually routed Elizabethport, N.J., to Scranton, Pa., train is the result of the CNJ abandoning its operations in Pennsylvania but retaining a traffic gateway in Scranton via a pool agreement with the EL. And for you smart alecs who think this is eastbound SE-98, consider that this is the light power from ES-99 making a switching move—the blue SD40 is the lead unit, note that there is no engineer in the cab of Red Baron 3067! (*CNJ Baldwins*, BOYD; *all others*, BALL)

74

Transition on the Jersey coast. Undoubtedly, the joint Pennsylvania–Jersey Central operation of the New York & Long Branch has been one of the most colorful in the New York area over the years, continuing into Penn Central, Conrail, and Jersey DOT. My buddy Walt's backyard goes to the railroad's property line, and through him I have gotten to know the railroad, its crews, and, yes, its independent spirit. In a sampling of color, above, two Conrail Geeps take EL-1 up Middletown Hill en route to Lakewood on April 10, 1978. At left, engineer Russ Clayton and fireman Bill Bilarczyk wheel train No. 3307 through the Cliftwood curve in December 1978. At upper right, Penn Central's prettiest train, in my opinion, the *Rustoleum Limited*, crosses the Red Bank bridge on December 1, 1972. At lower right, CNJ's—rather Conrail's, make that NJ DOT's—train No. 5313, locally called *The Bay Head Builder* for its array of ex-GN, NP, and BN cars, heads out of South Amboy on May 4, 1978, looking for all the world like a refugee from the Burlington Northern merger. (BALL, WALT GROSSELFINGER–BALL COLLECTION, BALL, BALL)

The 460 miles of multiple-track main line between Boston and Washington are now officially called the Northeast Corridor. On the New York–to–Washington leg, the rails are so busy I've nicknamed it "the shooting gallery," as trains continuously shoot by at speeds approaching—and often surpassing—the century mark. I have walked thousands of miles of railroad tracks throughout this country, and the corridor is the only railroad I feel uneasy being around.

Historically, the Boston–to–New York segment was completed in 1876, linking with the Pennsy via transfer steamer between the Bronx (New York City) and Jersey City. "Centennial Trains" between Boston and Philadelphia were inaugurated on May 8, 1876, the trip taking 12 hours (including the two-hour boat segment). From steam, through electrics, low-center-of-gravity *Keystones*, the *Congressional Limiteds*, *Metroliners*, and today's E60s, the New York–to–Washington run has hosted America's fastest trains. Indeed, John Barriger claimed that the primary reason American railroads were not nationalized during World War II was because the Pennsylvania Railroad didn't collapse from the strain—much of the credit going to the electrification and the unbelievable number of trains that could be accommodated. In later years, of course, we have become familiar with the corridor on a national basis, with all the hoopla that followed the High-Speed Ground Transportation, Research and Development Act in 1965, and, ironically, it was the Northeast Corridor that, in my opinion, saved Amtrak!

And where do you catch the high-speed action? Better *here* than Philadelphia. On this page, top to bottom, the ageless G heads the list. This is February 23, 1978, and GGI #910 sails on through Torresdale, Pa., exceeding 100 mph, pinch-hitting for a Metroliner. In the middle, and Washington-bound like the G above, an E60 comes off the Elizabeth, N.J., curve with the *Congressional* on February 9, 1978. Below, a set of vintage MP54s pass the Union Tower, Rahway, N.J., en route to South Amboy on March 30, 1973. Highball! On the right, two extremes in electrics: "Old Rivets," America's first GG1, in its "glow in the dark" Conrail Bicentennial paint and EMD's experimental GM6C electric. The 4800 was shot in Enola, Pa., in April 1976, while the GM6C was tying onto a piggybacker across the river near the Harrisburg depot in June of that year. (*GM6C*, BOYD; *all others*, BALL)

UN-SNAFU! Resplendent in its traditional Pennsylvania Railroad Brunswick green, gold pinstripes, and red keystones, Amtrak GG1 #4935 heads up a National Railway Historical Society special at Safe Harbor, Pa., on October 30, 1977. When a group of railfans offered to raise funds to repaint a GG1 into its Pennsy livery as a tribute to these greatest of American electric locomotives, Amtrak's president Paul Reistrup gave his enthusiastic support. Amtrak immediately caught the spirit of the project and selected their #4935 for the honor—the 4935 was one of the last GG1s owned by Amtrak to retain its original PRR number and to have unmodified air intakes, thus making it as historically authentic as possible.

A group calling itself "Friends of the GG1" solicited funds, and Amtrak's Wilmington shop forces overhauled the loco-

motive and did the actual paint job. World-famous industrial designer Raymond Loewy—the man who restyled the GG1 for the PRR back in the 1930s from a rivet-laden hulk into a sleekly welded classic—was on hand for the dedication and "autographed" the 4935 with a penned signature on its flank. Rather than a static museum piece, the 4935 became a piece of living history as it resumed its place in Amtrak's regular motive power pool, generally catching assignments on the *Broadway* or *National Limited*, and becoming one of the GG1s upgraded for Metroliner substitution service— and, of course, being on call for special events or excursions. As the 4935 rolls up the "Port Road" along the Susquehanna River and beneath the massive trestle of the Atglen freight line, her Amfleet consist confirms that even a federal bureaucracy can have a heart. (BOYD).

3

BLACK DIAMONDS, BLACK DIESELS, BLACK INK

AMERICAN FREEDOM TRAIN FOUNDATION
AUTO-TRAIN CORP.
BALTIMORE & OHIO RAILROAD CO.
BESSEMER AND LAKE ERIE RAILROAD CO.
BUFFALO CREEK & GAULEY RAILROAD CO.
CASS SCENIC RAILROAD
CHESAPEAKE AND OHIO RAILWAY CO.
CHESSIE SYSTEM
CLINCHFIELD RAILROAD CO.
CONSOLIDATED RAIL CORP. (CONRAIL)
EAST BROAD TOP RAILROAD
GEORGIA NORTHERN RAILWAY CO.
GEORGIA PACIFIC LUMBER CO.
GULF, MOBILE AND OHIO RAILROAD
ILLINOIS CENTRAL RAILROAD
LOUISVILLE AND NASHVILLE RAILROAD CO.
MARY LEE RAILROAD (U.S. PIPE & FOUNDRY)
NORFOLK AND WESTERN RAILWAY CO.
PENN CENTRAL TRANSPORTATION CO.
PENNSYLVANIA RAILROAD
PITTSBURG & SHAWMUT RAILROAD
RICHMOND, FREDERICKSBURG AND POTOMAC RAILROAD CO.
SEABOARD AIR LINE RAILROAD CO.
SEABOARD COAST LINE RAILROAD CO.
SOUTHERN RAILWAY CO.
TENNESSEE, ALABAMA & GEORGIA RAILWAY CO.
TENNESSEE CENTRAL RAILWAY CO.
TERMINAL RAILWAY ALABAMA STATE DOCKS
UNITED STATES ARMY TRANSPORTATION CORPS
VIRGINIAN RAILWAY CO. (N&W)
WESTERN MARYLAND RAILWAY

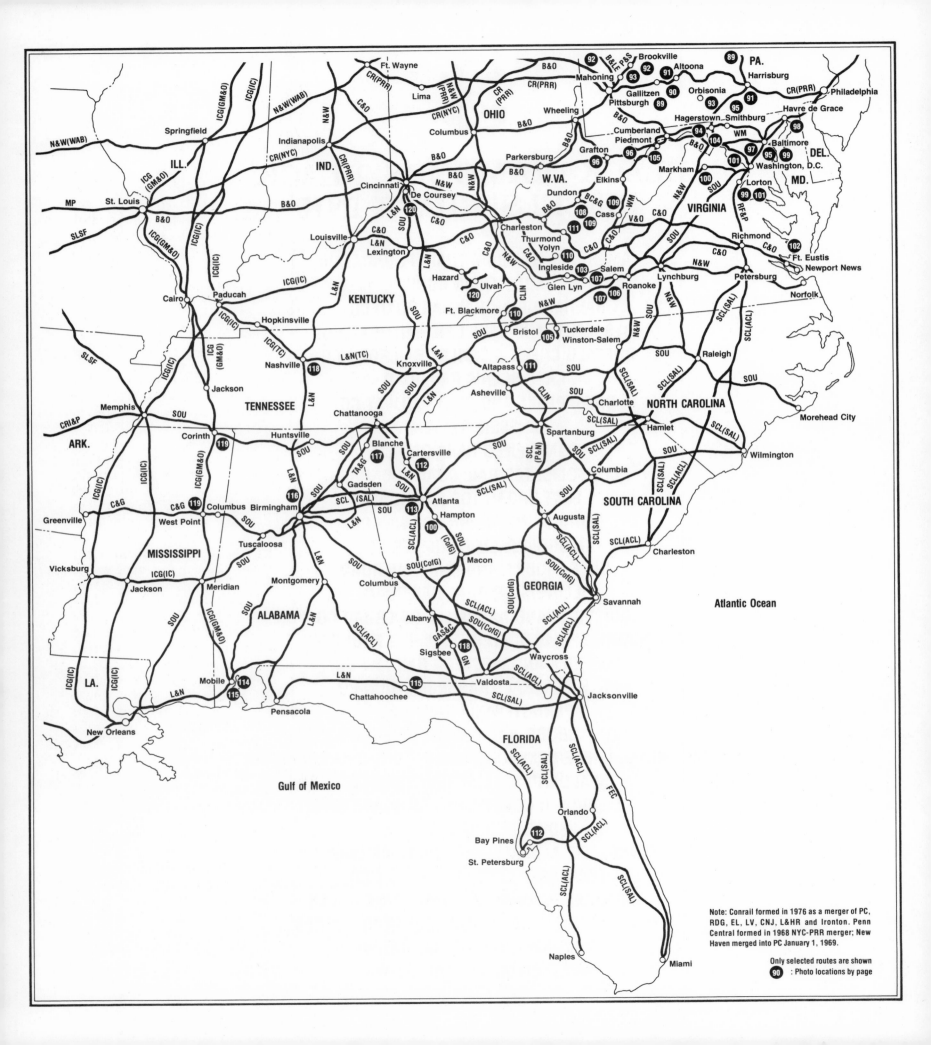

Note: Conrail formed in 1976 as a merger of PC, RDG, EL, LV, CNJ, L&HR and Ironton. Penn Central formed in 1968 NYC-PRR merger; New Haven merged into PC January 1, 1969.

Only selected routes are shown

90 : Photo locations by page

IN PAST BOOKS, I've talked about my love affair with the Buffalo, Creek & Gauley Railroad in Dundon, W. Va.—a coal-hauling road that did not dieselize after all the big brethren did, and operated in some of the most beautiful country in America. What I *have not* talked about are the trips down to West Virginia—the erratic routings, top down on the sports car, up for 30 hours-at-a-clip nonsense that was all a part of younger years. I laugh when I pull out a road map now (or several of 'em) and remember trying to explain that Altoona was, somehow, on the way from New York to Dundon! I marvel at the fact that I could call a buddy on Thursday night, take off from work at, say, three o'clock on a Friday, and be back—physically, at least—at my desk on Monday or Tuesday, having taken in much of Pennsylvania and West Virginia in the interim!

On one incredibly clear, warm Indian summer evening, Walt and I pointed the car west on the Pennsylvania Turnpike, headed, so we thought, on a direct run for the Buffalo, Creek & Gauley. We knew the drive time was 18 hours, taking into account the winding, mountainous roads after we got off the Pennsylvania Turnpike at the Bedford exit. By the time we crossed the Susquehanna, the sun was sending blades of orange and gold light across the deep blue-to-apple-green sky, turning the layers of feathery clouds fiery red. It was one of the most spectacular sunsets I've ever seen. As the colors deepened, the sky got brighter—so bright, in fact, that I pulled the car off the road to shoot some color exposures. Behind us, a full harvest moon appeared in the deepening sky. On this beautiful evening I knew I could drive on and on indefinitely. We were now an even hundred miles from Exit 11 at Bedford and that moon, WWVA, some rotten jokes, and the lovely top-down evening would make the miles fly. On the westward trek along the Pennsylvania Turnpike, we encounter the mountains around Newburg; with Blue Mountain, Kittatinny and Tuscarora tunnels slicing right through the backbone of the Appalachians. The next two hours of turnpike driving continue through and along the mountains, but we're going to exit in another few miles at Bedford.

Now this is 1962 and my dedicated hatred of diesels is well known to Walt. An 18-hour, straight-through drive to see a 2-8-0 lugging coal should be sufficient evidence of my love for steam. Why, just the thought of seeing a steam-powered revenue freight gave me the adrenalin to keep driving, and Walt knew this. After all, what could be more rewarding than a sunny, early morning rendezvous with steam, down in the beautiful mountains of West Virginia. I'm reminded of Steinbeck, who wrote of the "virus of restlessness" that often takes possession of men, and when it does, "the road away from here seems broad and straight and sweet," the victim first having to find in himself "a good and sufficient reason for going." The last few miles of turnpike driving turned into philosophizing: How one man can long for mountains without even being their child. How another man yearns for the city, another for the plains. We laughed at a mutual friend back home who loved the sea and joked about his conviction that he would end up in hell, for the Bible says that in heaven "there shall be no more sea." Bedford. Downshift to third; to second; reach for ticket and money. Time to stretch and have some coffee.

First stop after the toll booth is a nearby diner. Coffee-counter conversation consists mostly of a series of laconic grunts from Walt. I know something is bothering him. "Do you know how far we are from Horseshoe Curve?" he asks.

"Horseshoe! What the hell are you saying?"

"Less than an hour away," replies Walt.

"What are we here for? What about the Buffalo Creek?"

Walt counters: "I think it would be worth seeing some big trains and catching the Centipedes!"

Premonition. Call it what you want. It was already 10:00 P.M., and I decided to call BC&G's general manager and friend Rich Manning about Saturday's and Monday's schedule. "Looks like neither" came the answer. "Are you coming down?" A moment of silence and Rich continued: "We'll be going Sunday, can't make it tomorrow; I'll explain when I see you." Realizing the Kentucky & Tennessee Railroad was too far for a quick trip, I opted for the Curve—and a night in a motel.

Horseshoe Curve . . . I was trying to think back on when I was last at the Curve. Was it en route to see B&O steam one time? Was it on a drive back from Chicago? I was there for the last J-1 class 2-10-4 operations, but I remembered being there since. In the motel, I was clearly thinking of the time I climbed up the steep steps from the gift shop to trackside on the middle of the Curve, when three Geeps approached, working a westbound merchandise train up outer track 4; 100 or more cars later, two oily, grimy Baldwin Centipede diesels came into view, shoving on the cabin car. I remember that I laughed at the pathetically huge multiple-wheeled (48 of 'em) machine, looking for all the world like a big, dumb animal, plodding along. The bruiser moved—burbled—on past me with slow deliberateness, seemingly on stiff legs. As it headed into the curve, I could have sworn it was wearing olive-drab trousers! That impression really stuck. My interest was captured by the various chomping, growling noises the thing emitted—even after it had passed from sight. I remembered how quickly the air grew colder as the sun moved behind the mountain and, as it set, how the surrounding sweep of mountains took on dramatic proportions in the cold, low light. It was fall, late fall, when I was last at the Curve. I know I even waited for my amusing Centipede friend to drift back down the hill, clomping away at every rail joint. I remembered calling it "Flops"; somehow it reminded me of a basset hound! Before I left, a man came up and joined me for a few minutes of conversation. He told me the Centipedes were "tired old bulls." Now, clearly, as I contemplate the Curve I remember actually having anxieties over whether the Big Baldwins would be culled from the herd before I could stop by again. Tomorrow is that "again," and I hope they are still there. I went to sleep that night in the Bedford Motel trying to remember when—and why—I last stopped by at the Curve.

Morning dawned bright, and the mountain air was every bit as clear as I expected it would be. Fog, really mountain mist, started to collect in the valleys from the sun's warmer rays. We played nip and tuck with the dense fog along Route 220, dropping down into the gray murk and climbing back out, over and over again. The local radio stations called for nice weather, but the mountain air can be tricky and weather unpredictable. By the time we reached Altoona, high, feathery wisps of cirrus clouds were prevalent—not a good sign. Out over the mountains, low layers of gray stratus clouds were moving in, and I knew something the weathermen apparently did not know.

Now, diesels not withstanding, Altoona has to rank as *the railroad city* in the United States—even in 1962. During World War II, locomotive construction shops spread over 218 acres in a 126-building complex that was manned by 13,000 workers. Aside from these largest-in-the-world shops, Altoona was one of the busiest division points on the railroad. Seldom were any of the four mainline tracks quiet. The weather did close in, and Walt and I went to either Alto Tower or Slope Tower, just west of Altoona Station, to introduce ourselves. (I regret that after steam disappeared I stopped taking notes, drawing interlocking plans, and writing down names.) My objective was to try and get a ride up the mountain in one of the Baldwin Centipedes I had laughed at what I believed to have been two years earlier. "You're too late," said the operator. "We're all new hood units on the rear end now." His words brought back the days when ops told me I had just missed the last such-and-such steamer I was looking for. "The Baldwin junkers fell apart and died—we got Alcos now."

The speaker crackled and three hood units reverberated by, rattling the tower windows with a westbound coal train. Soon the train slowed to a crawl, and the operator got on the horn to notify the enginemen that their rear had cleared the west switches. Much to our surprise, the operator notified the helper that "two gentlemen will be riding with you up the mountain and back." "Roger" came the reply. I was amazed! No IDs, pass, hardhat. Nothing that suggested we were railroad brass. And this is the railroad that threw me out of Grogan Yard, Columbus, six years earlier for taking a picture of an I-1 on the table!

My on-the-job introduction to second-generation railroading began with the two new boxy-looking Alco units clattering through the crossovers and stopping next to us. We climbed aboard, and introductions were quickly made. The fireman was our "instructor."

We are told we are aboard an Alco AS-18am (Alco Roadswitcher, six axles, mu-equipped) known more commonly as an RSD12, the second (lead) unit being identical. I quickly find out that this is not the Pennsy I watched two years ago, close to the time the last first-generation GP9 entered PRR road service, New Year's week, 1960. The brass in Philadelphia were beginning a buying spree, the biggest part of which was going to all three builders for the second-generation hoods. We couple on, a full brake test is initiated and soon the air hisses through the trainline. "Brakes applied and released. Pressure is 80 pounds." The head end replies, "Roger."

"We're going, Skipper." 3,600 Alco horsepower throb, and we move into the rear end of our train to take up slack. "Highball!" comes from the head end, and from now on, it's careful teamwork—watching what the head end is doing, listening on the phone for brake-pipe reductions, watching the ammeter and wheel slip light. The Alco shakes from the beating of its four-stroke 251 engine; the ride, a hard, heavy-on-the-rail feel. The fireman tries to explain Alco's Tri-Mount truck, telling me it's a one-piece casting without a separate bolster. He glances up our long, black train of hoppers and continues telling me about the Tri-Mount, while a rough rider, gives the truck stability against rising, and tends to load the wheels more evenly, preventing axle lift. "We have to watch the wheel sizes on these engines; a worn wheel in a lead position will climb the outer rail!" I wasn't sure what he meant, but I felt comfortable watching the engineer's concentration—as if he were in constant mental contact with the guys up in the haulers (Pennsy's term for road engines). The whamming Alcos! If man even bolted together a machine that sounded as if it would self-destruct at any moment, this is it! We're down at 10 miles an hour, and our engineer radios the head end. I cannot hear the reply. "We're good at 6 miles an hour but the head end isn't," the fireman yells to me. More conversation and I find out that the maximum pulling power that can be achieved without overheating traction motors for the EMDs on the head end is 11 mph. We keep shoving, but at once I suspect that more than one roasted traction motor has been caused by Alco helpers slogging along at under 10 mph!

Now Horseshoe comes into view as part and parcel of the entire shove up the mountain. Our engineer salutes the cold K-4 steamer on display with two quick blasts of the air horn. The relentless beat of the Alcos continues, each cycle of every piston stamping and shaking the floor in the cab. The smell of warm oil is heavy, the heat from the engine clearly felt. The ever-climbing railroad seems to be one long curve to the left, followed by another, and another. The grinding, whamming "chong chong chong" beat of the engines goes right through my body. In a few miles, we're suddenly in an echo chamber, surrounded by the roar of the Alcos. "Top of the grade," shouts the fireman, and all I know is that we are in a tunnel. "We're comin' up on AR Tower and our cutoff man." We are out into the world again and we slow to a stop. The contented offbeat chant of the idling Alcos gives no hint of the work we just did. Why, Alcos always sound as if they are going to die with the next stroke (couldn't resist that one!).

After cutting off, we head around a 180-degree loop and back past AR. "Clear." The fireman attempts to explain dynamic braking as we drift back down the mountain. From AR to UN and Benny, we are in a timing circuit, going down the mountain. An engine or train cannot pass through the circuit below a certain time or a whistle will be set off and the engine or train will be stopped. This precaution was put in after the *Red Arrow* ran away down the mountain many years ago, killing scores of people. Back toward Altoona, we encounter an approach signal. "Slow Clear," shouts the fireman, looking down at a pot (dwarf signal) sitting next to the tracks. "Slow approach . . ."

Oh, yes, on the Baldwins. The fireman confirmed everything I had expected—such gems as their being built with a separate radiator for cooling the oil, that was placed over the electrical cabinets so that every wire became an instant wick from dripping oil! Gems like the cooling blower connections to the traction motors always getting out of line and cooling the ballast . . . the fuel tanks being an integral part of the car body and always leaking . . . the fact that the PRR determined their locomotive costs per mile in cents, with the exception of the dollars-plus-a-mile Centipedes. The fireman looked up at me for a moment and remarked, "We never went up the mountain with all four engines; I wonder why the damned things never did us the favor of having two engines or all four crap out at the same time!"

I opened this chapter mentioning the Buffalo, Creek & Gauley Railroad and West Virginia—two of my favorite subjects. In all my past books, I've romanced about the steam on the BC&G and the native beauty of West Virginia. It is ironic that because of steam, I got to know West Virginia, and by getting to know West Virginia, I became very disillusioned over what has broadly been called "government inequities."

In late 1960, when I made my first trip down to the Buffalo, Creek & Gauley, the sound of an N&W coal train in the hills had changed noticeably with the droning of diesels and bleating air horns. Nevertheless, coal trains had reverberated through the West Virginia hills since early statehood, and it was a healthy sound of the most vital transportation link West Virginia had with the rest of the nation. It was obvious that waterways, highways, and airways played a far less important role than the coal-hauling railroads in keeping West Virginia a dynamic factor in the American economy. And yet, my professional involvement in railroading was deep enough for me to grasp quickly the fact that West Virginia was helping the railroad competitors with one hand, while taking away from them with the other hand. I'll explain.

By the end of 1960, West Virginia had not made an equitable adjustment in its 27-year-old privilege tax on transportation. Railroads were paying at the rate of 4 percent, while motor carriers were paying 1.5 percent. The airlines were paying nothing. The result: the railroads were paying more than 90 percent of the total transportation privilege tax collected. In 1960, the railroads were only asking that all forms of transportation pay this tax at the same rate. Even then, of course, there still would not be full tax equality since the competing modes were either getting all, or at least the greatest portion, of their rights of way—highways, airports, and waterways—at taxpayer expense. The railroads, of course, provided their own rights of way.

In an interview with *Railway Age* in late 1977, Norfolk & Western president John P. Fishwick talked about the future of the N&W, the government's regulatory policies, and his railroad's government-bankrolled competitor, Conrail. I'd like to quote several paragraphs, in context, from this interview. Keep in mind we're now talking 1977, not 1960.

"I believe our biggest competitor is the government—and it isn't through support of Conrail.

"The government controls our competitive environment by providing highways and waterways for the use of trucks and barges and charges less than a fair amount, or nothing, for their use. It's the government that fixes the rules for our competition with the trucks. The federal government built the Interstate Highway System and it largely planned that system so that it is sufficient for big trucks. Hills are projected on a 3% grade, which is necessary for trucks but not necessary for automobiles. There are wider medians, wider lanes, thicker pavement to take care of the trucks. The trucks are presently increasing their weights; they're going to double bottoms. What we're really going to have is little trains running over the highway.

"Common-carrier truckers are protected from entry by competitors. But if they want to quit, they can quit—take their money and go home. If you're a railroad you can't do that. You've got to keep serving the public until you go broke. The common-carrier trucks have pretty much a monopoly over the small-packages business. But our real competition is the independent trucker. They can go out of business whenever they want to, they can charge what they want to, they can haul whatever is available. They can operate 150,000 or even 200,000 miles a year with one tractor. They don't make a great deal of money, but they set the standards of competition. So do the barge operators, with their free use of government-provided waterways. So the government is really our competitor."

Tempus fugit. . . .

Closing out the decade of the '70s, the skyrocketing price of oil has propelled the freight train to our national conscience and to the forefront of transportation planning for the next decade. In West Virginia and across the nation, coal trains are increasingly on the roll. So too, rail freight traffic is generally up while traffic for regulated truckers is declining. "It's premature to say that we've won a lot of traffic from the trucks, but demand has been steady and has continued to grow over the last 10 years," said Stanley Crane, chairman of Southern Railway, which has been touting the superior fuel efficiency of the rails in full-page advertisements. In 1977, Southern's freight traffic totaled 902.4 million revenue ton miles, up 5 percent from the year before.

It may be too early to predict a railroad renaissance—in the face of the railroad industry's labor and capital needs, estimated at $17 billion for modernization over the next few years—but it looks like we're off to a good start! We can always hope.

The second generation diesels on the Pennsylvania Railroad were about as spartan as anything on rails; two reasons for this were the ever-present thought of a merger with New York Central and not wanting a "flashy PRR image," plus the ease of merely exchanging decals when and if the merger took place. It turned out to be a good decision, but wouldn't it be nice to turn back time and photograph some of these "spartan diesels" we ignored!

Above, an Alco C425 leads a GP9 and a train of hoppers along the upper reaches of the Susquehanna River near Renovo, Pa., in the early spring of 1965. At immediate right, two Alco DL702s shove a heavy coal train up the 1.8-percent ruling grade from Altoona to the summit at Gallitzin on October 4, 1962. In another mile, the long train will stop and the helpers will be cut off to return back down the hill to 17th Street on the west side of Altoona, where they will immediately be assigned to another westbound. (MARTIN ZAK, BALL COLLECTION, BALL)

Pennsylvania Railroad into Penn Central and into Conrail...no matter what the name, the railroading is very much the same out over the Alleghenies—rough! I, for one, quickly forget that diesel railroading *can* be exciting. I long to hear a steam locomotive, down to a crawl, slamming its deliberate exhaust into the sky and it's not until I encounter the likes of Horse Shoe Curve that I realize railroading is still very exciting. Listen, sometime, as two high-horsepower diesels approach on the rear of a heavy train, nursing—pushing—the reluctant cars. With welded rail, the click-clack of wheels is gone, but the groaning cars stubbornly resisting the push is a sound you'll never forget! Like hogs being driven—herded—to market! At left, it's July 1, 1976; Conrail is exactly three months old. The action is the sheer drama of getting symbol PR-9 up around Horse Shoe and over the Alleghenies. At upper right, the scene is repeated, but back in Penn Central days, and before the welded rail. Below, two SD45s move slowly toward the Rockville Bridge with a transfer run out of Enola. The date is July 2, 1976. (BALL, BOYD, BALL)

Pennsylvania is a beautiful place to experience autumn, especially if you like to mix your "leaf looking" (as the natives say) with train watching. With locomotive colors matching the foliage, a pair of Bessemer & Lake Erie Alco DL600s, right, are shoving hard on the rear of an ore train nearing Albion, Pa., in October 1968; while in October 1973 a trio of Pittsburg & Shawmut SW9s, below, are lifting a string of empty hoppers over Red Bank Creek just outside of Brookville, Pa. That same weekend, the Shawmut was playing host to Steam Tours' ex-Reading 4-8-4 #2102, below right, still wearing its disguise as Delaware & Hudson 302, an alteration made earlier in the year to help the D&H celebrate its 150th birthday. The friendly little Shawmut provided a splendid setting, and the "302" never looked better than she did striding over that curving trestle near Mahoning.

Even after the last golden leaf has departed, Pennsylvania still presents one annual steam attraction to liven up a long, bleak winter: the Railfan Winter Spectacular held every February at the East Broad Top in Orbisonia. In February 1976 three narrow gauge Mikados bound a full tourist train into the crisp afternoon cold, far right, departing Orbisonia.
(BOYD, DONAHUE, BOYD, DONAHUE)

I often wish my writing could be the product of spontaneity—relating my exact feelings at the time of an event. How can I explain why, after seeing countless Reading T-1s in regular service and on fantrips, I was so thrilled at the sight of ex-Reading #2102 running light into the Hagerstown engine terminal after her February 5, 1972, fantrip from Baltimore? 2102's entrance was not a performance, rather just plain railroading; simply a light engine coming home after a hard day's work. Somehow a T-1 never looked better. At upper right, Western Maryland symbol AJ-3 appears under a leaden sky, heading through Smithsburg, Md., on February 4, 1972, behind a mix of EMD and Alco power. Below, and on a quiet Thanksgiving Day 1967, a sampling of WM's handsome first-generation diesels idle away in Ridgeley, W. Va. At lower right, American Freedom Train's #1 is fired up, sans skirting, in Baltimore's Riverside Yard on April 25, 1975, after her complete restoration. (BALL, BOYD, BALL, BALL)

The nation's first true railroad, chartered in 1827, the Baltimore & Ohio pushed beyond its initial Baltimore–Ellicott's Mills segment all the way to Chicago and St. Louis. The soul of the B&O, however, remained in the Allegheny Mountains, at places like Grafton, W. Va. In December 1967 the baggage carts are rattling down the platform at Grafton, right, to service the head end cars of No. 11, the *Metropolitan,* bound from Washington to St. Louis. The lone coach attests to the train's success as a passenger accommodation, but the matched A-B E8s and vintage clerestory-roofed baggage cars make a timeless scene in front of Grafton's elegant depot and imposing Railroad YMCA Hotel.

After listening to the diesels laboring wide open for a solid hour clawing up Seventeen Mile Grade, it's an odd sensation to feel the sound die away and the speed pick up as the train crests the hill and begins to roll down Deer Park Grade on the other side. The *Advance Cincinnatian,* below right, is beginning to ramble down Deer Park in November 1967 as it meets a Fairmont coal train howling uphill behind a trio of SD35s.

The B&O's premier passenger train is the *Capitol Limited* between Baltimore, Washington, and Chicago. Gracious service and punctual performance are a B&O tradition right down to the end. On May 1, 1971, the day of Amtrak's implementation, the last *Capitol* comes bounding across historic Thomas Viaduct on the south side of Baltimore dead on time, far top right.

By its 150th birthday, the B&O has been merged with the C&O into Chessie System, but that new corporation is not about to overlook its heritage. To celebrate its sesquicentennial, the *Chessie Steam Special* was created, using Ross Rowland's ex-Reading 4-8-4 #2101, former *American Freedom Train* #1, for two years of systemwide excursions. One of the most colorful steam trains ever assembled, the *Special* is westbound over Thomas Viaduct, far bottom right, on May 12, 1978, bound for Cumberland and a weekend of tackling two of the B&O's most famous grades, Sand Patch and Seventeen Mile. (BOYD, BOYD, BALL, BALL)

Three generations of railroading—in the 1970s. Author David L. Cohn talked of the South possessing qualities that appertain to no other region of the country, qualities that are "largely survivals, real or fancied, of the antebellum traditional South carrying over into our times: the wistful past, staining with faint Tyrian purple the white fabric of the present." Cohn's prophetic remarks come keenly to mind, watching a Canadian Pacific Royal Hudson steaming south across the Susquehanna River at Havre de Grace, Md., on February 2, 1979. A CPR 4-6-4 heading down the B&O for deepest Dixie, seemingly heading for a never-never land, an earthly Elysium. At upper right, the implications are easier to grasp, watching four Southern Railway F7s hurry the Atlanta-bound *Piedmont* out of Washington and across the Potomac into Virginia on April 14, 1976, under the watchful eye of Jefferson. At lower right—"with Tyrian purple the white fabric of the present"?—we are watching Auto-Train's impressive ribbon of purple, red, and white bearing down upon RF&P's main line behind GE U36Bs through Woodbridge, Va., nearing its northern destination at Lorton. The date is April 8, 1975. (COLLECTION—WALT GROSSELFINGER, BALL, BALL)

Southern talk that's sweeter than honeysuckle and bourbon emanates from the stacks of the numerous steam locomotives the Southern Railway continues to operate over its 10,000-mile system. Southern's hospitality comes in big measure, too, as witness the two scenes depicting present-day operations, at left—operations that proudly keep the Grand Era alive. SR's most celebrated engine, Mikado #4501, is pictured, at top, passing through the lush Virginia countryside near Bellemead, en route to Front Royal on July 21, 1974. Below, spritely Consolidation #630 puts 'em up and lays 'em down heading through a *Gone with the Wind* setting in Hampton, Ga. on a break-in run prior to the next day's *Georgia Peach Special*. That's Southern's president W. Graham Claytor, Jr., at the throttle of the 630. They're on the CofG headed from Atlanta to Griffin. Only the auxiliary water canteen gives away the date as being June 1969 instead of 1939, but frankly, my dear, I don't give a damn!

At upper right, and certainly sweeter than coal smoke at Southern's executive offices, four immaculate high-nosed EMD's greet the morning sun, heading a hotshot north through lovely back country near Clifton, Va., on November 20, 1974. Much can be, and should be, said about the Southern and the fact that it is a darned successful rail enterprise, even in these days of misery for so many other railroads. Southern's car loadings continue to be way over the national average. Revenues climb to all-time highs, net consolidated income soars, and return on net investment tops the industry. Southern's operating ratio is taut when compared with other railroads, and the amount of money poured back into plant and equipment improvements routinely sets industry records. *Fortune* magazine ranks Southern number one among the railroads in earnings-per-share growth. Why the continued success? Maybe because they believe in the *railroad*.

At lower right three Richmond, Fredericksburg & Potomac EMDs scorch the ballast, "wheeling the pigs" north toward Potomac Yard on April 8, 1975. The location is Woodbridge, Va., and that long-end-forward configuration of the lead unit is definitely not typical of the RF&P. (*#630,* BOYD; *all others,* BALL)

I entered the '60s finishing up my army tour in the 714th Railway Operating Battalion as an Instructor of Railway Operations at Ft. Eustis, Va. Instead of carrying an M-1, I carried my TM55-20 (Railway Operating Rules) and Time-table No. 7, effective 0001 Hrs. Sunday 25 May 1958 (which was still in effect in 1960). Hanks Yard, James Yard, Trecom Spur, Wagner, Patton, King, Wye Tower, Chessie, Miles and Mulberry Switch were all part of my Army lexicon, as were 2-8-0s and 0-6-0s. I remember actually being embarrassed trying to explain my tour to others, after my discharge! In a nutshell, "I had it made" in the army. In 1960, it was commonplace to wake up in the wee hours and hear a steam engine calling for a movement through Wye Tower, or leaving Hanks, heading for the James River Sub-Division. My favorite engine at Ft. Eustis was 0-6-0 #614. She fired well, was "gutty," as we used to say, and more important, whistled like a Burlington 0-5! She's pictured, at left, returning to the shop ready track, after making up a troop

102

train for Dripping Springs Rifle Range. Ah, such was (army) life!

The *real railroad story* of 1960, of course, was the absolute and final dieselization of the Norfolk & Western—the last major railroad in the U.S. to discontinue steam. I have *tried and tried* to document the last steam assignment of the N&W, to no avail. Best guess is a Y-6b out of Williamson, W. Va., on the Pigeon Creek Shifter on May 6, 1960. My last steam-chasing trip on the N&W and into the coal-blackened hollows along the railroad was in March 1959. The Y-6, at upper right, westbound at Glen Lynn, Va., was made on this trip, on March 18.

N&W stepped from steam right into hood units, not being interested in diesels when all the other railroads were ordering first-generation cab units. The typical post-steam train is pictured at lower right, behind a horde of Geeps—in this case, climbing toward Ingleside, W. Va., en route to Bluefield in January 1970. (BALL, BALL, BOYD)

Total recall. When First-96 highballed past the Shomo Yard limits toward Hagerstown behind a bulking Y-6b...when a streamlined K rushed No. 13 out of town toward Shenandoah...when CV-60 whistled off and headed for Harrisburg...when Western Maryland ganged up enough Consolidations to run up Williamsport Hill. Total recall: Ex–Nickel Plate #759 bringing forth wonderful memories, storming south out of Hagerstown on the N&W on April 24, 1972, with 50 some odd freight cars. Highball!

A pair of Norfolk & Western Geeps has replaced the traditional 4-8-0, and an International steel caboose rolls along in place of a Tuscan red combine, but other than that, the Abingdon Branch is much the same in April 1974, top right, as it was in 1954. The rambling and rustic branch

from the N&W's main line at Abingdon, Va., to isolated West Jefferson, N.C., has been a favorite with railfans for decades because of its rural charm and timeless character. Don't mind that the train runs across your front yard, they only come through Tuckerdale on Tuesdays.

It's big-time railroading at its best as Chessie System and vintage B&O EMD's drop a coal train down Seventeen Mile Grade through Luke, Md., and across the North Branch of the Potomac River into Piedmont, W. Va. On this late afternoon in May 1976, below right, the eastbound coal train is leaving an unmistakable trail of blue brake shoe smoke in its wake as composition shoes and the diesels' dynamics strain to keep the tonnage under control. (BALL, BOYD, BOYD)

Wildlife species are passing from the scene all over the country. The heath hen and the passenger pigeon are gone. The wolf and the condor are relics that exist only in the most restricted of ranges. The disappearance of a species is something unheralded, almost unnoticed. So, too, many railroads are passing from the scene—some virtually relics that exist only with infusions of state and federal funds until time runs out; others, strong, but not as strong as their neighbors. The Virginian Railway Company certainly fits into the latter category, but neighbor Norfolk & Western was just a bit stronger.

With Norfolk & Western steam attracting my attention in the 1950s, there was little thought of watching the nearby Virginian. Virginian is now N&W, of course, but the magnificent "bridge architecture" of the VGN is still very evident today. I wish I had paid more attention.

At immediate right, an N&W hotshot powered by an impressive array of engines heads west into the mountains near Elliston, Va., on October 29, 1978. The Alco C630 and ex–Virginian Train Master slug are heavy-duty yard engines working their way to an assignment on the Bluefield hump. The yellow circle on the black square next to the ACI label on the Train Master slug is a bit of a mystery. It is a "U-1 wheel stencil" that was required on a slug (pardon the pun) of freight cars as part of an inspection program searching out potentially faulty 33-inch wheels made of an improper fracture-prone steel. Once the wheels were inspected, the U-1 stencil was applied. Since no locomotives were involved, one would have to assume someone got carried away. The picture below was taken just a few miles east of Elliston on the Virginian in 1958, but the electrification continued after the 1959 N&W merger and into the early 1960s— there was *no way* this beautiful 6,800-horsepower brute was going to miss appearing in this book! At upper right, and standing waist-deep in the Roanoke River to get the shot—in October, yet—a quartet of N&W Geeps head east over the old Virginian with hoppers in tow, through Glenvar, Va., on October 31, 1978. At lower right, eastbound merchandise roars through Glen Lynn with an SD45 in the lead. That's the old Virginian main line crossing the New River in the background. (BALL; COLLECTION —EUGENE VAN DUSEN; BALL, BOYD)

From everywhere rises the scent of somnolent leaves and decaying leaves—for the earth is getting mellow. The scent rises over the West Virginia hills and down in the valleys, steaming up aspiringly under the warm October sun, tinting the air with its moist incense. From across the creek another scent noses in, as slight as a mist and as intangible as a dream; a sun-kissed smell in the hazy air; a wonderful smell we had become accustomed to in West Virginia. We walk across the railroad bridge that spans the creek and come face to face with a pair of idling B&O GP9s, but our suspicion is right. Buffalo Creek & Gauley 2-8-0 #14 is at the Dundon interchange much earlier than expected, pumping her train, throwing her tantalizingly assertive breath around in the air.

Above, and later that same October 1962 day, Georgia Pacific's Shay #19 returns through Swandale, over the BC&G. At lower right, Cass Scenic Railroad's Shay #2 poses for about three dozen photographers on the former Mower Lumber Co. railroad, now turned tourist hauler. The occasion is the Annual Railfan Weekend; the year, 1975. (BALL, DONAHUE, BOYD)

Racing like a Piedmont 737 on takeoff, the Clinchfield Railroad's 1882-vintage 4-6-0 #1, above, sprints southward near Ft. Blackmore, Va., headed for Erwin, Tenn., with a trainload of excursionists on May 10, 1969. The pride and joy of general manager Tom Moore, #1 is used on excursion trains and Santa Claus specials. More typical of Clinchfield operation is a loaded coal train dropping down "The Loops" below Altapass, N.C., behind two SD45-2s and a U36C, above right, in April 1973. Coal keeps the Appalachian economy moving, and the Chesapeake & Ohio is one of the biggest coal movers in the area. In May 1969 the "Rum Creek Shifter" with a pair of C&O Alco DL702s shoves a string of empty hoppers past the Island Creek company store at Yolyn, W. Va., left toward Amherst's MacGregor Mine. Deep in the New River Gorge, right, a C&O Geep idles on the main line in front of the ancient wooden depot at Thurmond, W. Va., in the summer of 1973. (BOYD)

A train seldom looks more impressive than when rolling over a deck trestle. There's that constant sense of amazement that a one-inch wheel flange can keep hundreds of tons of hardware from plunging into space. The rumbling of an E8 on Louisville & Nashville's No. 3, above, is a temporary disturbance to the placid Etowah River just south of Cartersville, Ga., one morning in June 1969. Filling the schedule of the old *Georgian*, nameless No. 3 originates out of Evansville, Ind., and provides token overnight service to Atlanta, as the L&N struggles with the governmental agencies for its discontinuance.

Similar in consist to L&N No. 3, Seaboard Air Line No. 5 carries the description "Passenger, Mail & Express" in its timetable listing. After slowing for the Emory University flagstop, No. 5, far right, traverses a timber and steel trestle on the north side of Atlanta in February 1965. At right, a timber trestle of different proportion supports a Seaboard RS3 rolling the boxcars of a local freight across an inlet at Bay Pines, Fla., in 1964. Like many roads, the Seaboard had dramatically different freight and passenger paint schemes. Although it is not evident in the photo at far right of No. 5, the "white" E8 #3051 is actually a very light mint green—truly! (BOYD, COLLECTION, BALL)

The genteel Gulf Coast city of Mobile, Ala., is also a bustling seaport and quite a focal point of rail activity. The nucleus of Mobile's port and industrial trackage is owned by the Terminal Railway of the Alabama State Docks. In August 1968 a brand-new SW1500 has the afternoon "country job" in tow heading inland for the International Paper mill and Alabama Power steam plant. Departing North Docks Yard, left, it negotiates a working swing bridge over a navigable inlet off the Mobile River. The TRASD's crimson and white colors honor the University of Alabama, but half of the railroad's fleet is painted orange and blue for Auburn!

Shortly after midnight on a warm August evening in 1968, at right, a workman is hosing off the windows of the L&N E7, on train 8-11, the combined *Pan-American* and *Gulf Wind,* as it makes its station stop in Mobile. The New Orleans–to–Cincinnati *Pan-American* carries the through sleepers and coaches for the New Orleans to Jacksonville, Fla., *Gulf Wind* as far as Flomaton, Ala., where they are switched out to make up a separate train. The *Gulf Wind* travels on L&N tracks as far east as Chattahoochee, Fla., where the Seaboard Coast Line takes over. Several months earlier, an SCL E7 was idling the night away, below, at Chattahoochee after handing over the westbound *Gulf Wind* to the L&N. It will take over the eastbound *Gulf Wind* at 9:10 A.M. and carry it on to Jacksonville. (BOYD)

Birmingham has the Baldwins, the countryside the TA&G. In September 1969 the steel city of the Southland was home for some of the country's rarer locomotives. With only subtle exterior details revealing that they have lost their lusty but outmoded four-cycle 1600-h.p. Baldwin diesels in favor of more reliable 1750-h.p. EMD 567Cs, a pair of black and boxy Baldwin AS616s idles at the fueling facility, upper left, in the midst of United States Steel's huge Fairfield Works. Over on the other side of town, however, the original gutsy Baldwin engines are churning out their rpms inside former Missouri Pacific AS16s, below left, now working for the Mary Lee Railroad Division of U.S. Pipe & Foundry. In striking new orange paint, the trio of Baldwins kicks up the dust entering the grounds of the pipe plant after making a run down from the mine about 20 miles north of Birmingham.

Among the true treasures of American railroading are the small regional railroads—not short lines, but small railroads that have the tonnage and trappings of a big system condensed into a compact and understandable size. Up North you think in terms of the Green Bay & Western; Toledo, Peoria & Western; or the Monon. But in Dixie nothing typifies the regional carrier better than the Tennessee, Alabama & Georgia. With four of the railroad's five locomotives working on one train, GP18 #50—named the *David E. Hedges* in honor of a former company official— disturbs the dust at a rural crossing near Blanche, Ga., above, on the daily run from Chattanooga to Gadsden, Ala., in June 1969. With two unnamed GP7s and GP38 #80, the *John A. Chambliss,* speeding the tonnage southward, the TA&G presents an image as businesslike as any of its bigger neighbors. I, for one, now know what railroad my next model Geep is going to be painted! (BOYD)

It was the EMC FT diesel freight unit of 1939 that vanquished the steam locomotive, but looking at the faded glory of Georgia, Ashburn, Sylvester & Camilla #16, at left, you'd hardly suspect this bell-bedecked tramp of rural Georgia to be of such grand heritage. By January 1968 when #16 was seen here rambling northward on the Georgia Northern through Sigsbee, Ga., she was one of the very last FTs running anywhere.

On the same trip, the lights of Nashville, Tenn., were creating a nocturnal glow in the clouds of a growing snowstorm as Tennessee Central RS3 #249, below left, idled the night away. Once Reading's #508, the #249 was one of the few units to receive the TC's new blue and gray colors.

At upper right, Gulf, Mobile & Ohio arrives with a trainload of pulpwood and merchandise behind a perfectly matched Alco FA1-FB2-FA1 set, at Corinth, Miss., from Memphis in June 1965. The first FA1s built, the GM&O units are unique in having their headlights positioned below the "roll" of the nose and by wearing the stylish curved grille behind the cab door otherwise found only on the PA passenger units.

The first buds of spring lace the trees in West Point, Miss., below, as a black Illinois Central GP9 heads south toward Jackson in March 1971. Spring's torrential rains are not very far behind.
(BOYD, BOYD, BALL, BOYD)

Deep in the valleys of the eastern Kentucky coal fields, a pair of Louisville & Nashville Alco C420s, right, pick up some loaded hoppers from a tipple at Ulvah, Ky., on the Rockhouse Creek branch as a farmer with his tractor waits for them to clear the crossing. It's April 1974, and the first green on the trees promises relief from a cold and hard winter. When their loads are gathered, the Alcos will trundle their way west and north to the yard at Hazard, where the hoppers will become coal trains and heavy road power will lug them northward to Cincinnati. A few years earlier, in July 1968, a handsome FA2-FB2-FA2 set of L&N Alcos, below, was gathering momentum with another coal train north out of DeCoursey Yard headed across the Ohio River with a transfer run into Cincinnati. (BOYD, BALL)

4

FARM/CITY

AMTRAK
ATCHISON, TOPEKA AND SANTA FE RAILWAY CO.
BURLINGTON NORTHERN INC.
CHICAGO & ILLINOIS MIDLAND RAILWAY CO.
CHICAGO AND NORTH WESTERN TRANSPORTATION CO.
CHICAGO, BURLINGTON & QUINCY RAILROAD CO.
CHICAGO GREAT WESTERN RAILWAY
CHICAGO, MILWAUKEE, ST. PAUL AND PACIFIC RAILROAD
CHICAGO NORTH SHORE AND MILWAUKEE RAILWAY
CHICAGO SOUTH SHORE AND SOUTH BEND RAILROAD
DETROIT, TOLEDO AND IRONTON RAILROAD CO.
DULUTH & NORTHEASTERN RAILROAD CO.
DULUTH, MISSABE & IRON RANGE RAILWAY
ERIE LACKAWANNA RAILWAY
FAMILY LINES SYSTEM
GRAND TRUNK WESTERN RAILWAY
GREAT NORTHERN RAILWAY
GREEN BAY AND WESTERN RAILROAD CO.
GULF, MOBILE AND OHIO RAILROAD
ILLINOIS CENTRAL RAILROAD
ILLINOIS TERMINAL RAILWAY CO.
LAKE SUPERIOR & ISHPEMING RAILROAD CO.
LOUISVILLE & NASHVILLE RAILROAD CO.
MINNEAPOLIS & ST. LOUIS RAILWAY CO.
MONON RAILROAD
NORTHERN PACIFIC RAILWAY
NORTHWESTERN STEEL & WIRE
PENNSYLVANIA RAILROAD
SOO LINE RAILROAD CO.
SQUAW CREEK COAL CO.
TOLEDO, PEORIA & WESTERN RAILROAD CO.
WABASH RAILROAD CO.

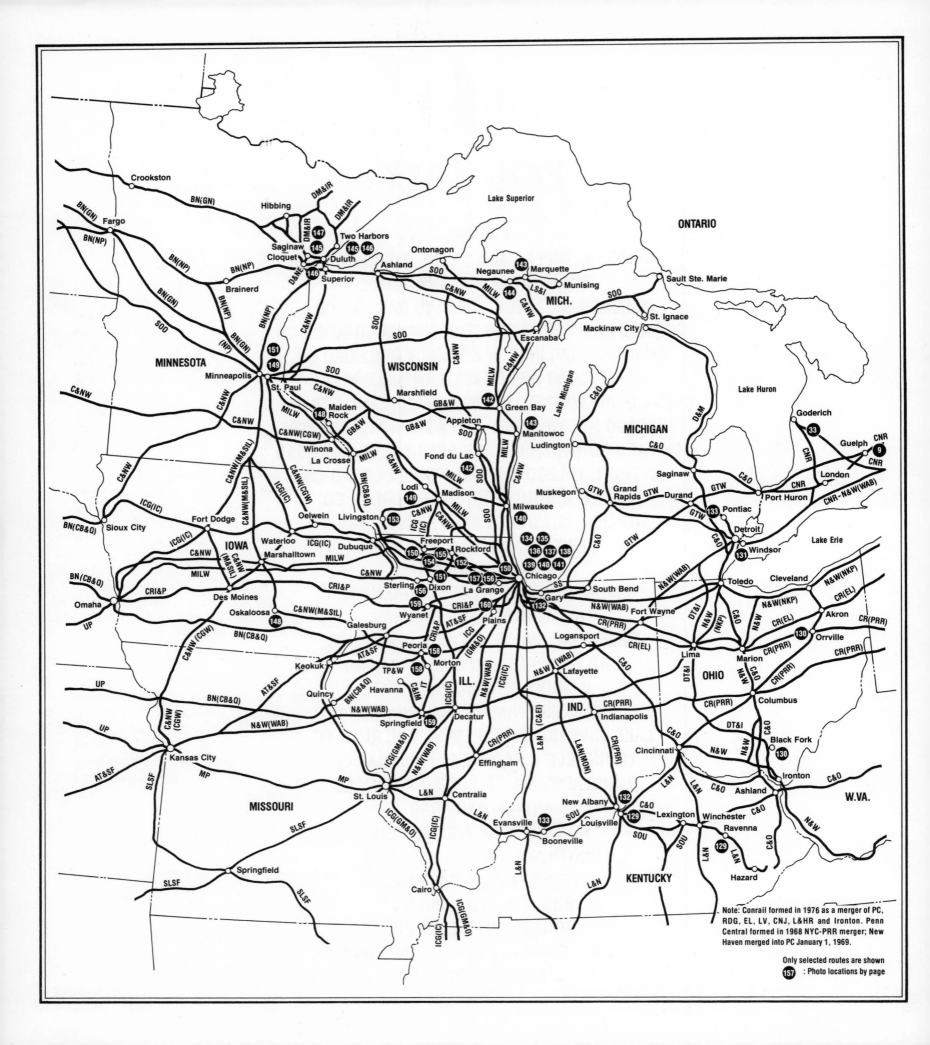

Crookston

BN(GN)

Fargo

BN(GN)

BN(NP)

DM&IR

Hibbing

DM&IR

ONTARIO

Lake Superior

BN(NP)

BN(NP)

BN(NP)

Brainerd

BN(GN)

(NP)

BN(NP)

Saginaw

(147)

Cloquet

(145)

Two Harbors

(146)

(146)

Duluth

Superior

Ontonagon

Ashland

SOO

Negaunee

(143)

Marquette

C&NW

MILW

(144)

Munising

Sault Ste. Marie

LS&I

MICH.

SOO

MINNESOTA

(151)

(149)

Minneapolis

St. Paul

C&NW

WISCONSIN

SOO

Escanaba

C&NW

Mackinaw City

St. Ignace

Lake Huron

SOO

Marshfield

C&NW

GB&W

(142)

Green Bay

MICHIGAN

Goderich

(33)

C&NW

(148)

Maiden Rock

GB&W

Appleton

Guelph

CNR

(9)

CNR

MILW

SOO

Manitowoc

CNR

C&NW(CGW)

Winona

La Crosse

GB&W

MILW

Fond du Lac

(142)

SOO

Ludington

C&O

Saginaw

C&O

London

CNR

ICG(IC)

MILW

C&NW

Lodi

(149)

Madison

MILW

Muskegon

GTW

Grand Rapids

GTW

Durand

GTW

CNR-N&W(WAB)

Port Huron

C&NW(M&StL)

BN(CB&Q)

MILW

Milwaukee

(140)

GTW

(133)

Pontiac

BN(CB&Q)

Sioux City

ICG(IC)

Fort Dodge

C&NW(M&StL)

Oelwein

Livingston

(153)

ICG(IC)

C&NW

SOO

GTW

Detroit

(131)

Windsor

Lake Erie

ICG(IC)

Waterloo

Dubuque

Freeport

(134) (135)

Rockford

(136) (137) (138)

IOWA

Marshalltown

MILW

(150)

(154)

(155)

(152)

(139) (140) (141)

C&NW

C&NW(M&StL)

(151)

(157) (156)

(150)

Chicago

South Bend

N&W(WAB)

Toledo

Cleveland

N&W(NKP)

C&O

N&W

Sterling

Dixon

La Grange

SS

Gary

CR(EL)

Akron

CR(PRR)

BN(CB&Q)

MILW

Des Moines

CRI&P

Omaha

UP

Oskaloosa

(148)

C&NW(M&StL)

Wyanet

(159)

CRI&P

(160)

Plains

AT&SF

ICG

N&W(WAB)

Fort Wayne

CR(PRR)

Logansport

CR(EL)

C&O

Lima

DT&I

N&W (NKP)

C&O

Marion

N&W

CR(PRR)

(130)

Orrville

CR(PRR)

BN(CB&Q)

Galesburg

Peoria

(158)

Morton

(158)

ICG (GM&O)

Lafayette

C&O

N&W (WAB)

OHIO

CR(PRR)

Columbus

UP

AT&SF

Keokuk

TP&W

ILL.

ICG(IC)

N&W (WAB)

Indianapolis

C&O

DT&I

C&O

Quincy

BN(CB&Q)

Havanna

C&IM

IT

N&W(WAB)

Decatur

CR(PRR)

IND.

CR(PRR)

N&W

N&W

Black Fork

(130)

UP

BN(CB&Q)

N&W(WAB)

Springfield

(159)

L&N (C&EI)

L&N(MON)

Cincinnati

N&W

C&O

Ironton

C&O

Kansas City

MP

MP

ICG(IC)

Effingham

CR(PRR)

L&N

L&N

C&O

Ashland

W.VA.

C&NW (CGW)

AT&SF

L&N

Centralia

L&N

New Albany

(132)

C&O

Lexington

Winchester

C&O

N&W

SLSF

MP

St. Louis

ICG(GM&O)

Evansville

(133)

SOU

Louisville

(129)

Ravenna

(129)

SLSF

MISSOURI

ICG(IC)

L&N

Booneville

SOU

L&N

L&N

C&O

SLSF

Springfield

SLSF

Cairo

ICG (GM&O)

KENTUCKY

Hazard

ICG(IC)

Note: Conrail formed in 1976 as a merger of PC, RDG, EL, LV, CNJ, L&HR and Ironton. Penn Central formed in 1968 NYC-PRR merger; New Haven merged into PC January 1, 1969.

Only selected routes are shown

(157) : Photo locations by page

CHICAGO, CHICAGO, what a tottling (railroad) town! Chicago. A city coveting the gentility of the East, yet determined to remain the hog butcher of the world. A place of propriety as well as sin; of stardust and sawdust. Chicago. A city of extremes; while waiters in hunting-pink coats and black-satin knee breeches scurry obsequiously about the Pump Room of the Ambassador East, strip teasers strut down the runways of rancid honky-tonks along West Madison and North Clark streets. Chicago. Brown in the south, white in the north, with the iron-bound Loop in the middle. State Street, that great street—from Benjamin Franklin's Variety Store to Marshall Field & Company. Chicago, with its blue-green lake to the east and brown-gray neighborhoods and factories to the west—a prairie boom town, stretching forever. From Stoney Island to the Near North, a city of striking contrasts. From South Shore to *Super Chief,* IHB and NYC, Chicago is the place to be.

When you're dealing with or within a specific time frame, such as I am doing with this book, there is always that inevitable tug to "go back once more" and compare what was with what is. Nineteen sixty is our starting point. I would like to, once again, return to this year.

As the decade opened, the Illinois Central was boasting of "encouraging gains" in passenger service. Overall, IC passenger revenues were up more than $1 million over the year before. The Post Office increased its service over IC's Iowa Division—enough to enable the western lines (as IC folks say) to take on a "new healthy glow." A condition set by the P.O. for giving the IC the business was that the *Hawkeye* had to depart from Chicago for Sioux City an hour earlier than its regular schedule called for. The IC did one better, changing the *Hawkeye's* departure time to 90 minutes earlier, and knocking 30 minutes' running time off the schedule! At the same time, Flexi-Van mail service was inaugurated on the *Land o' Corn* between Chicago and Waterloo, connecting with a special mail train over the remaining 100 miles, nonstop to Fort Dodge. E6 diesels highballed both containers and passengers close to the Century mark, and the world never looked so good!

In 1960, IC's principal trains— the *Panama Limited, City of New Orleans, Louisiane, City of Miami,* and the *Seminole* were all operating in the black on an out-of-pocket basis. Three Northern Pacific vista domes were leased and tried on the *Panama Limited* and *City of Miami.* They were successful, and a decision was made to continue the domes as a regular winter-season feature on both trains. The road operated some fall-foliage specials in southern Illinois, carrying record loads. On one trip, the railroad had to turn 1,500 people away! Even the *Green Diamond,* the last IC train on the Chicago–St. Louis run, had a healthy increase of patrons, despite its early afternoon departure from St. Louis and the more frequent competing service operated by the Wabash and GM&O. For passenger-train watchers, the IC had one of the best shows around Chicago.

While mail—and passengers—were riding the IC's Iowa trains, rival Milwaukee's *Sioux* was discontinued in January 1960, followed closely by C&NW's total discontinuation of its Chicago–Council Bluffs passenger trains. In retrospect, I'd love to know how much, if at all, these neighboring train-offs helped IC. One thing helped—IC's president Wayne A. Johnston was a firm advocate of the "passenger trains are here to stay" school. His conviction resulted in the freshly washed, spic-'n'-span fleet of matching orange and brown trains.

Well, what happened? Here's where we take that overall look at events—in this case, the total decline of rail passenger service—and draw conclusions. I was with ACF during the '60s and can share some of the intriguing forces and counterforces that were at work at the time. Specifically, in 1965, the Commerce Department and the New York Central got to work on the idea of trains carrying automobiles—*and their passengers in them!* I remember the ACF designs and the time engineers had, designing rest rooms and a snack bar onto a test car. In the beginning of 1965, mail revenues constituted almost 40 percent of C&O-B&O passenger revenues. As the parallel federal highways were completed, the Post Office took all mail off the two trains serving Ashland, Ky., Columbus, Toledo, and Detroit and diverted sizeable amounts of mail to trucks from C&O trains in Virginia and West Virginia. Paul H. Reistrup, then C&O-B&O director of passenger services, commented on the Post Office's actions: "I've asked it before and I'll ask it now. What's going to happen next Christmas or any time the Post Office needs us, and there are no trains in operation to move the mail swiftly and reliably?" Interestingly, the General Accounting Office reported to Congress that, in 1964, the Post Office Department had incurred unnecessary costs through the airlifting of first-class mail when reasonably adequate surface transportation was readily available. The GAO questioned whether the program gave adequate consideration to "the cost and reasonableness of the airlift service." The report stated that rather than a predicted cost reduction of $212,000 annually, the costs actually increased by about $1.1 million, approximately 85 percent more than the estimated surface cost. It also stated that the program was even used at times when existing surface transport could provide equivalent service at substantial cost savings. "Neither snow-covered highways nor ice-coated wings stays these couriers. . . ."

In the spring of 1964, Walt came out on the *20th Century Limited* from New York for a visit. I considered meeting him at Englewood (his suggestion) in hopes of catching the tails of both the *Broadway Limited* and *20th Century Limited* as they paused at the station. Why bother, I thought. I have mentioned my "dedicated hatred of diesels" earlier in the book. Nineteen sixty-four was just another year without regular steam operations, so the cameras were quiet. I met Walt at LaSalle Station and, yes, he confirmed that the *Broadway* was in Englewood. "What a shot!" he remarked. I gave it nothing more than passing thought. Walt had taken Friday off and had come, so I thought, for a day of Burlington steam with the double-heading 5632 and 4960 on a fantrip. Anything other than steam seemed to be on his mind, at least when he arrived. After an enjoyable 16 hours on a train, I thought to myself, one can be romanced easily by the railroad and not need yesterday's steam memories. The cruncher came when Walt whipped out a well-scheduled "shopping list" of trains he wanted to see. From Rock Island to B&O, *Kate Shelly* to *Thoroughbred*, Nickel Plate PAs to Soo Line F7s, Walt obviously knew the Chicago railroad scene and how he wanted to participate in it.

He was my guest this time, and we wasted no time getting out on the town—the railroad part of town. Walt had the right maps, official guide, individual schedules, notations on yard and enginehouse facilities, all the logistics on paper—and I didn't even bring a camera. My mind was on tomorrow and Burlington's fantripping 5632 and 4960.

I was also thinking of Chicago's spell—the fact that people and businesses still come there with the expectation that Chicago will be the best for them. When the city's boosters proclaim it "the town hall of the nation" or crime reporters declare it "the hooligan capital of the nation," and certainly when the railfans call it "the railroad capital of the nation," Chicago seems the best choice for better and for worse. Chicago was my home now, and outside of occasional dinners over at Rock Island's Track 1, and the few times we called Santa Fe to reserve dinner in the Turquoise Room to Galesburg, I really didn't know much about Chicago's railroads and trains any more. Steam obviously played an important role in my interest.

That Friday was cram-jammed with trains—and disappointments. Rock Island's diesels were now a solid maroon with white stripes, and C&NW's *Kate Shelly* had only three cars, and no diner. The F units had been bumped by Geeps on Soo's *Laker*, and the PA's were off the Nickel Plate. Even GM&O's "plug" had an RS-1 that day and Monon was now black and gold! As Walt and I came to grips with the present we witnessed a rather dismal array of trains and remnants of the past. Illinois Central, Santa Fe and Burlington "looked normal," and, true, there still were some long, slanted-prow diesels from the glamour era, but the dazzle was gone; the disappointments far outweighed the likes of IC, Santa Fe and Q. I was suddenly grateful for the few good grab shots I had previously taken of the now-gone passenger trains we were looking for. I had forgotten my encounter with the *Laker* behind F units several years ago; I had forgotten the beautiful Rock Island maroon and crimson *Rockets* I shot while waiting for steam, and I had forgotten the few red and gray Monon trains I shot while in college. Yes, I had even forgotten Nickel Plate PAs through Belleview while waiting for Pennsy J-1s. Not only did the second generation bring us total dieselization, hood units, and mergers, but drab, less costly paint schemes. That Friday taught me a lesson—get it while you can. After four year's abstinence from contemporary railroad photography, I realized how *quickly* the rail scene had changed. After Walt returned home, he continually prodded me to get out by the tracks and "take it anyway" as he would (and still does) say!

Over the next few years, some of the big name trains made the front pages and evening TV news feature stories as they highballed to oblivion. Trains like the *20th Century Limited* and *Phoebe Snow* were gone! I guess we shouldn't have been so shocked, since men like Southern Pacific's president Ben Biaggini had been speaking of the "enormity" of passenger-train deficits for several years, declaring the long-distance passenger train dead. Indeed, in the mid-'60s there was talk that the *City of San Francisco*, using the Milwaukee, Union Pacific and Southern Pacific, following the first transcontinental rail route, might not even be around to celebrate the 100th anniversary of the first transcontinental railroad in 1969. The passenger trains went through several years of indictments during the '60s and, in many cases, outright convictions. The trains that continued to run, coupled with our capacity for ignoring reality, somehow sustained most of us at trackside during the '60s. In 1970, the National Railroad Passenger Corporation was set up by Congress to combine a remaining number of passenger trains into a single, quasi-government-operated system. On May 1, 1971, Amtrak began operations of 182 passenger trains over 20 member railroads, serving 314 cities and towns on 20,600 miles of track. One hundred eighty-two passenger trains; that's 178 fewer trains than the day before. For the first time, Maine, New Hampshire, Vermont, Arkansas, South Dakota, and Wyoming were without passenger trains, and, perhaps even "more wrong," Cleveland was left without any passenger trains! In many states, there was now only one stop for one train a day and in roughly 40 of the city-pairs that had direct train connections, there was no more service. It was left up to regional government agencies to volunteer to assume the deficits if trains were to be put back on. The rest is history.

Since that epic May 1, 1971, I have ridden thousands of miles on Amtrak and one overriding question constantly nags me: What would happen if the government paid, say, 10 railroads that currently operate, or could operate, the "core" of Amtrak's service the same subsidies presently being dished out to Amtrak to run their train, or trains, under their own banner—in their own individual paint schemes/identities? I'm sure one element that I feel is currently missing within Amtrak would return: *pride*. I wonder what would happen?

As I write this, I'm thinking back to a few weeks ago, when I was in Chicago with just enough time on my hands to go over to Union Station to look at some trains. Through the doors facing south, the angular-shaped F40s looked in, their head-end power screaming decibels of defiance to noises long gone from Union. Their raging madness of power reminded me more of an airport, certainly, than of a station—and the uniformity of equipment may just as well have been an apron full of 727s and DC-9s. The emotions of history and self all ran together. It was a day, in T. S. Eliot's phrase, that mixed memory and desire.

So often we go back to what is past and unrecoverable in our lives. I contemplate all the trains I've taken out of Union Station; each train and journey was a totally different experience. With Amtrak, a microwave hamburger onboard the AmCafe on No. 22 across Illinois is the same as on No. 176 traveling the shoreline to Boston.

There is one pre-Amtrak train I would like to call attention to: a special train with a name of its own, a train that celebrated its Diamond Anniversary and received national praise from Washington. A named train that didn't even appear in the public timetable (though I'd speculate its schedule was adhered to as closely as any passenger train). I was not even aware of the train, nor its colorful history, when I had my first encounter with it.

I'd like to return to that 1964 three-day visit with Walt, and my perhaps cryptic comment at the time about his easily being romanced by railroading and not needing "yesterday's steam memories" to do so. On May 17, we spent the better part of the day relishing Burlington's big Northern #5632 and Mikado #4960 double-heading an excursion across Illinois. Both steamers whistled and stormed through our lives and all but snuffed out thoughts of present-day railroading. The chase by car was exhilarating, the run-bys (after we managed to get ahead) even more so. Certainly, any *other* trains that may have passed that day went unnoticed. Toward day's end we were full of steam, and that's what counted. The two locomotives pounded past with the present satisfaction that they were wonderfully alive; they stirred memories, too. For me, it could have been a big Rock Island M-50A working with a K-64 on a troop train through Lawrence. For Walt, a Santa Fe train his dad and he had ridden during the war. No matter, the pages on 20 years' worth of calendars amounted to confetti that day.

The world was right—that is, until the radiator hose went on my car. A rude, unhappy ending to a thousand yesterdays and a harsh re-entry into the present. The hose cost us the last two hours of sunlight—the remaining four hours of the steam outing. Luckily, we were in a town when the hose let go, so we left the car at the Pure station and had a leisurely supper while the hose was replaced. I have a thing about small Midwestern towns with their close residential streets whose houses hold porches and memories. Always a large lawn in front and an alley out back. There has to be a railroad that passes through, a grain elevator, hopefully some work, or bunk cars for a section gang, a depot, a Deere dealer, store windows to look at, a Methodist church, a small park, and, of course, an A & W root beer stand. We had everything—even a First and Elm Street—and Walt bore with me as I walked the brick sidewalks after dinner. The serenity took my mind off our problems that day, and East Washington Street seemed to ease things back to better years. Walt, coming from the East, liked the change.

Train chasing in the Midwest is always a "grid game" of taking parallel roads within sight of the tracks and 90-degree turns to intercept. If the railroad takes a diagonal, you're out of luck, unless you can see smoke or are a native. With steam fantrips, there are usually motorcaders who know the lay of the land. Our drive home was mostly back farm roads on a giant grid that would eventually lead us to Route 34 east.

Invariably, the pressure of time catches up, and that damnable schedule we go by hits us like a neon sign. I take the car up another 6 or 7 mph and switch on the brights. I tell Walt to watch the yellow signs and read 'em out loud; four eyes on the road are better than two—especially, when you're tired. Ahead, nothing but dark, punctuated by an occasional farm light. One of those right-angle curves comes up and we're nailed! We've encountered Burlington's main line near a small hamlet, and the highway flashers are going. The roar of thousands of diesel horsepower gets us out of the car to trackside *on the double*. The fast-approaching train is screaming! Horns blaring, Mars light blinding. No time to think. Four Es wham by, elephant style, splitting the dark. The impatient V-12s are buried by RPO cars, bags, mail storage cars—a dust-raising vision of heavyweights and silvers whamming the rail joints. Many more cars, markers, gone!

Train No. 29, the *Fast Mail*, left two stunned steam fans standing in the dark.

Whereas steam locomotives are comfortable in black, diesels demand colors, and from colors they derive much of their character. Take L&N C420 #1327, above, for example. Photographed at Ravenna, Ky., in May 1979, that shiny new coat of Family Lines French gray obviously has just covered up the contemporary L&N livery of gray with a yellow nose, and that bell on the short hood in its strap-iron bracket is an unmistakable giveaway to the knowledgeable locomotive fan that this particular C420 began life in Monon's black and gold. Three lifetimes played out in three color schemes.

There's an even more intriguing story in the picture at right of L&N RS3 #259 at Louisville in June 1964. The 259 wears L&N lettering and an L&N herald on its cab, but the paint scheme is that of Vermont's Rutland Railway. L&N 259 was former Rutland #203, one of nine RS3s that were sold to the L&N when the troubled Rutland abandoned in early 1963. By the time the L&N got around to repainting or retiring its Rutland units, the handsome green and yellow colors had been resurrected "back home" in Vermont by the creation of the Green Mountain Railroad. (BOYD, R. T. SMART–BALL COLLECTION)

With a name like "Detroit, Toledo & Ironton," one might conjure up an image of multiple-track main lines and heavy coal and ore trains endlessly feeding hungry open-hearth furnaces. In reality, the DT&I is a somewhat more modest servant of the Detroit automobile industry and maintains a respectable flow of industrial and agricultural traffic in western Ohio and southern Michigan. The southeastern end of the railroad into its namesake Ironton, however, is a picturesque branch line that snakes through the hills and hollows looking for an easy entrance into the Ohio River valley. The "Ironton Run" out of Jackson, Ohio, above left, is about 35 miles north of Ironton as engineer Charlie Ogan exchanges waves with B&O operator Ron Henderson at Black Fork Junction on May 1, 1969.

At left, it's November 18, 1967, and we're watching a Pennsylvania Railroad hopper train rumble eastward through Orrville, Ohio, with a new Alco C425 teamed up with a leased N&W ex–Nickel Plate RS11 and a Pennsy GP9. That's N&W's former Wheeling & Lake Erie main line between Toledo and Brewster on the bridge.

The Wabash has been part of the Norfolk & Western for almost two years as F7 #658 awaits assignment at Windsor, Ont., above, in September 1967, but the international boundry has buffered the shock of change. While the rest of the system is in a turmoil of new ideas and blue paint—such as the RS11 on that Pennsy train at Orrville—the Wabash Canadian main line between Windsor and Fort Erie is running as it always has, in splendid isolation. The traditional Wabash colors of red, white, gray, and blue are mirrored in the ocean-going freighter making its way northward in the Detroit River toward Lake Huron. The F7, built by General Motors Ltd. in London, Ont., specifically for use on the Wabash's Canadian line, will shortly be scurrying across southern Ontario at a mile a minute, carrying finished cars and auto parts to Fort Erie and Buffalo. The Wabash banner never looked more regal.
(BOYD, BALL, BOYD)

131

Odd man out. Now here's a spread that would drive a picture editor nuts! Everything belongs, for we are covering the 1960s and 1970s. At upper left, Chicago South Shore & South Bend's "Little Joe" #802 has picked up cars from Georgia Pacific Lumber and starts pulling west. The location is West Gary, Ind. The weather is West Gary, Ind.! The date: January 9, 1978. At left, Monon's hotshot No. 71 from Chicago (Hammond, Ind.) rumbles through New Albany, Ind., behind two Alco C628s spliced by an RS2m on March 15, 1965. Above, Squaw Creek Coal Company's ex–Santa Fe Alco DL600B "Alligator" has a roll on the hoppers south of Boonville, Ind., en route to the Alcoa plant in Yankeetown in May 1977. At right, Grand Trunk Western's 4-8-4 and 2-8-2 duo are nearing Pontiac, Mich., under February 18, 1960's dreary skies. The railroad endeared itself to railfans in early 1960 by dispatching a daily hotshot out of Detroit to Durand behind double-slotted steam! Ironically, the Motor City played host to the grandest steam show in the United States in the 1960s. From yard service to symbol freights, local runs, and passenger trains, the GTW dispatched steam until late March 1960. (*Squaw Creek*, BOYD; *all others*, BALL)

Chicago is rightfully considered the railroad capital of the world, and there's no better place to catch passenger-train activity than 21st Street Tower where the leads to Dearborn and Union stations cross. With an upgraded RS2 in the lead and a rare old red-and-gray baggage car up front, Monon No. 5, the *Thoroughbred* to Louisville, is accelerating southward on October 17, 1964. At the same location but on a different track, one of the Pennsylvania Railroad's two afternoon commuter trains to Valparaiso, Ind., also accelerates uphill, with a GP7 leading a vintage pair of P70 coaches, left, in September 1965. Note the difference in exhaust between the Monon Alco and the Pennsy EMD. As usual, the Alco is coughing black, while the EMD blows blue.

From beneath the rusting trusswork and corrugated sheeting that make up the trainshed of Dearborn Station, a pair of handsome E8s have the Erie Lackawanna's *Lake Cities* in tow, at right, departing on a day-and-a-night trek to Hoboken, N.J.

Folks would probably never recognize the station if somebody should paint out that timeless landmark, Lee Work Clothes billboard! (BOYD)

"Ladies of Chicago." Over a century ago, the *Chicago Daily Journal* declared that bustling trade was transforming Chicago into the heart of America. "Our streets present an animated picture. Thronged with laden wagons, filled with busy people, vocal with the rattling of wheels, the rush of steam, the clank of machinery and many voices, goods gaily flaunting from awning posts and store doors, docks piled with boxes, bales and bundles of merchandise, warehouses like so many heart ventricles receiving the grain on one side, and with a single pulsation pouring it out on the other into waiting vessels and steamers to be borne away on the general circulation."

For now, not the magical land of southwest enchantment. Not the mountains and deserts of California, nor a region of Indian nations that conjures up mystical visages of Indian warriors, medicine men, and spiritual symbols. No, Santa Fe, in her prettiest of dresses has come to Chicago—to the din and dirt of the bustling town—as much a part of Santa Fe as the desert and the mountains. We sometimes forget. Above, the *Grand Canyon Limited* at 21st Street; at upper right, the *Texas Chief* beneath Clark Street; at lower right, the *Super Chief* at Dearborn; all Ladies of Chicago. (BOYD, BOYD, BALL)

Once again, Chicago. The city where more trains start and stop than any other on the globe; the city that keeps the jaws of the nation moving with chewing gum and gave taxi cabs of the world yellow jaundice; the city where the five-o'clock shadow starts at noon; the city that reversed the flow of its river. The vast terrain is industrial and gray, where a first impression can give you a hazing that leaves you meek, ready to settle on the farm, in the mountains, or in a New England village of white-painted houses. Chicago is a city bound by rails and the daily comings and goings of commuter trains.

At left, Rock Island's re-engined DL109, Christine. Dear Old Christine always looked like a wide-angle distortion when viewed normally. Jim couldn't resist a 28mm lense on her—and by the looks of things, neither could Christine! At lower left, would you believe the *Angelo Patria Andy Sardinia!* BN's E9 #9921, formerly #9991, has been named for a commuter in a railroad contest. *Angelo* is pictured heading into Union Station on August 10, 1973. At upper right, the early morning sun penetrates the canyons of Chicago on October 2, 1971, as a Chicago & North Western train heads out for the Galena Division. The Wisconsin Division splits off toward the north on the far tracks. At lower right, the 5:16 express to Midlothian departs LaSalle Station on the Rock Island on October 2, 1971. (*621*, BOYD; *all others*, BALL)

On a Sunday afternoon in October 1962, the 2:00-o'clock *Electroliner,* above, rolls down Fifth Street through the south side of Milwaukee. This North Shore Line interurban streamliner will terminate in downtown Chicago.

A real favorite among the faithful is *The Plug,* the Gulf, Mobile & Ohio's quaint commuter to Joliet. In 1964, left, it is approaching 21st Street drawbridge with two heavy-weight coaches and a genuine "chicken wire" F3 diesel.

In their glory years, the Union Pacific's proud streamliners, the *City of San Francisco, City of Los Angeles, City of Denver,* and *City of Portland,* each entered Chicago on the tracks of the Milwaukee Road from Omaha as a separate train, but by May 1970, all had been combined into one mammouth streamliner dubbed the *City of Everywhere.* Behind a quartet of E9s, the *City* departs the north side of Union Station, above right.

On May 1, 1971, everything changed when Amtrak took over. On that first morning of Amtrak operation, at right, the Amtrak *City of New Orleans* behind ICRR E8 #2021 and the Amtrak *South Wind* behind #797, the L&N's newest E8, await departure from Chicago's Central Station. (BALL, BOYD, BALL, BOYD)

'Tis said there are but two seasons in the "North Country," August and winter. That may explain why all the photos seen here were taken in August. Above left, in 1973, a twilight August sun is peeking under darkening skies at Fond du Lac, Wis., to illuminate a Chicago & North Western "cheater" Baldwin working the yard. Recently acquired by the C&NW, #1494 began life in 1951 as Baldwin AS16 #136 of the Missouri-Kansas-Texas, but it was re-engined with an EMD 1500-h.p. 567C diesel in 1960. Although outwardly unique, the re-engined Baldwins are internally good old reliable EMDs.

Handsome colors and well maintained Alco diesels make the Green Bay Route a pleasure to encounter any time, and the proud profile of an FA1 at the Green Bay roundhouse in August 1964, below left, is a true photographer's prize. The worldly railfan will take delight in pointing out that the 503 carries the initials of the Kewaunee, Green Bay & Western, the "paper" subsidiary of the Green Bay & Western Railroad.

With the rails creaking and its trusty Alco 244 engine rumbling contentedly, Lake Superior & Ishpeming RS3 #1608 skirts the shore of its namesake lake, above, as it enters Marquette, Mich., with the local freight from Munising on a shimmering, cool August day in 1972.

One year later, a Soo Line F7, right, is idling the day away on the turntable lead at Manitowoc, Wis., after bringing a "boat train" down from Neenah. A Soo Geep has just finished loading the freight cars onto the nearby Ann Arbor car ferry *M. V. Viking,* from whose deck the photo was taken. The *Viking* will carry the Soo railroad cars plus a handful of private automobiles and passengers across Lake Michigan to the Ann Arbor Railroad's port facility at Frankfort, Mich. (BOYD, BALL, BOYD, BOYD)

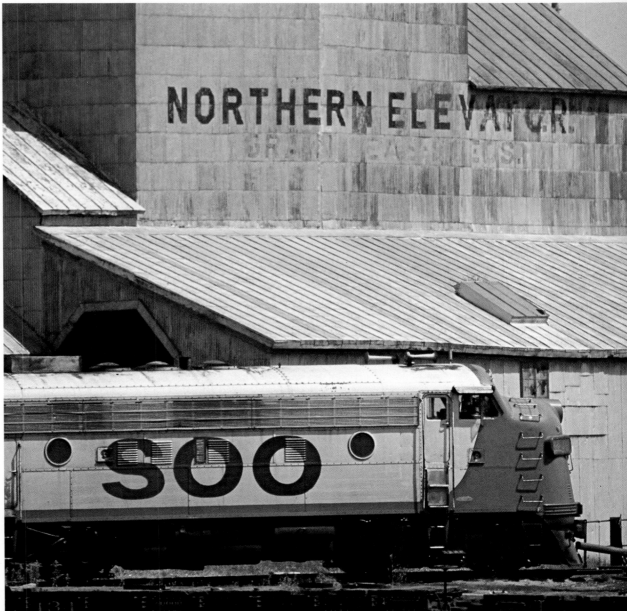

With their massive opposed-piston engines drumming authoritatively, a trio of Chicago & North Western Fairbanks-Morse H16-66 "Baby Train Masters" lifts an iron-ore train out of Negaunee, Mich. bound for the ore docks at Escanaba in August 1972. Although styled identically to their big brother 12-cylinder 2400 h.p. Train Masters, the C&NW's Babies are slightly shorter and pack only eight-cylinder, 1600-h.p. engines.

By the early 1970s railfan photographers were flocking to the iron-ore country to find the exotic locomotives, like the Baby Train Masters, that were still working there, but good diesel action photography of a decade earlier is more difficult to find, as most railfans virtually abandoned the area when steam died in the late 1950s. Although typical of the scenes found there in the early 1960s, the two photos at

right were taken in the late 1950s by photographers who reluctantly snapped off throwaway shots of unwanted diesels while waiting for Duluth, Missabe & Iron Range 2-8-8-4s to show up. The handsome Great Northern A-B-A F3/F7 set was on lease to the DM&IR in June 1959 as it neared the Duluth & Northeastern interchange at Saginaw, Minn. The DM&IR was replacing its huge steam locomotives at the time with a fleet of EMD SD9s and SD18s (plus a half-dozen Alco DL600s that were quickly transferred to sister U.S. Steel road Bessemer & Lake Erie). Below right, with the blue waters of Lake Superior in the distance, a pair of DM&IR SD9s was carefully dropping downhill toward the port facility at Two Harbors, Minn., on July 6, 1957. This train had steam the day before. (BOYD, DONAHUE, BALL)

The Duluth & Northeastern carried pulpwood and paper products in and out of Cloquet, Minn., behind steam power right into the early 1960s. The D&NE rostered a pair of delightfully ancient saturated-steam 2-8-0s, #14 and #16, two bigger and more modern-looking but actually older 2-8-0s #27 and #28, plus a gangling U.S. Army 0-6-0. Nearing the DM&IR interchange at Saginaw with the northbound morning train, #16 whistles for the highway crossing, right, in May 1960.

On Labor Day weekend 1962, the Illini Railroad Club ran an excursion on the DM&IR behind 2-10-2 #514, left, that included a stop at Saginaw and a run over the D&NE behind #27. On June 15, 1963, the American Short Line Railroad Association had a tour of the D&NE in a modern DM&IR caboose tacked onto the rear of the regular morning train down from Saginaw. Because of the special move, the D&NE did something it almost never does: it turned the engine at Saginaw and ran it downhill facing south instead of the normal tender first. (BALL, BOYD, DONAHUE)

"Where nature smiles 400 miles" is how the CB&Q bills its magnificent main line between Chicago and Minneapolis that spends the greater portion of its mileage hugging the east bank of the Mississippi River. Amid the autumn colors of October 1967, CB&Q No. 21, the *Morning Zephyr*, is speeding northward, left, near Maiden Rock, Wis. The passengers aboard the Northern Pacific's *North Coast Limited*, below, who are just getting ready for breakfast as the train nears St. Paul Union Depot, will soon be getting the same view as their train is forwarded down the CB&Q for its last lap into Chicago. The date here, though, is June 1968.

Affectionately known as "The Louie," the Minneapolis & St. Louis has already become a part of the Chicago & North Western, and in March 1962 the photographer was lucky to get a matched set of "reds" plowing a little snow, below left, through Oskaloosa, Iowa, with three EMD Fs bracketing a GP9.

17,000 gallons of beer?!? Sorry, Charlie, that Schlitz sign on the tender of Dick Jenson's ex–GTW 4-6-2 #5629 is only there to identify the sponsor of the annual Old Milwaukee Days circus train bringing the wagons for the parade into town from the Circus World Museum in Baraboo. Probably the most dazzling railroad consist to roll in the past two decades, the circus train is shown on the C&NW near Lodi, Wis., on June 30, 1967. (BOYD, BALL COLLECTION, BALL, R. T. SMART—BALL COLLECTION)

Below, on September 30, 1964, a perfect A-B-B-B-A set of Chicago Great Western Fs is right on time with the eastbound meat train No. 192 barreling through Dunbar (South Freeport), Ill. A little over two weeks later, on October 17, 1964, the autumn colors are more advanced as a pair of Milwaukee Road Fairbanks-Morse 1600-h.p. C16-44 "C-Liners" team up with an SD7, at left, to ease a freight from Milwaukee into Bensenville Yard on the north side of Chicago.

Chuggin' and luggin', that's what they built Baldwins for, and the Milwaukee liked to keep a number of them around the Twin Cities area for transfer work between the Pig's Eye Yard south of St. Paul and destinations around Minneapolis. A long grade out of the Mississippi River valley is part of the westbound haul, and in August 1966, below right, a trio of AS616s, the "hill Baldwins," are churning their way up the incline.

At immediate right, the Chicago & North Western's little hotshot freight 152 out of Belle Plaine, Iowa, was a favorite of the local train watchers along the northern Illinois main line for its often unusual motive power. A splendid example is this September day in 1966, with two rare RS3s—including the one and only RS3 in the experimental all-green paint—following a GP9 on 152 cresting the hill just east of Dixon, Ill. (BOYD)

While it's the main lines that make the money, it's the branch lines that serve the countryside. After laying overnight in Lancaster, Wis., less than 100 miles west of "home" in Madison, the Chicago & North Western's "Ridge Runner" has been rolling since the first light of dawn and is now headed southward near Livingston on the spur to Cuba City in September 1971, above. Just eight years ago GP30 #820 was the hottest thing on the main line, but an early victim of the horsepower race, it's been quite literally "put out to pasture" by a horde of SD40s.

A big engine but light on its feet, Milwaukee Road "SD10" #546 is a product of West Milwaukee Shop's program of modernizing older SDs for branch line and local service. Above left, on a hot and hazy morning in August 1975, engineer Mike Carlson is about to begin the day's work at Davis Junction, Ill., on the "Davis Junction Patrol," the main-line local. Below left, almost a decade earlier, in 1965, the night through freight from Janesville, Wis., to Ladd, Ill., is pictured setting off and picking up cars at Davis Junction. Typical power on the Ladd line in the 1960s was Fairbanks-Morse H16-44s, like #428 and #434. Interestingly, earlier that evening the train had passed through Beloit, Wis., within sight of the F-M factory where these locomotives had been built back in the mid-1950s. (BOYD)

There's nine thousand, eight hundred and fifty horsepower jumping across this spread! Although lacking the high-density action found on the Main Line of Mid-America south out of Chicago, the Illinois Central's lines west to Iowa and spreading through northern Illinois give a good representative sampling of what the railroad has to offer. Wearing the same regal colors as the *Panama Limited,* the more workaday *Land o' Corn* to and from Iowa carries the mail and passengers with equal dispatch, and although the "legal" speed is about 80, one may rest assured that 100-mph running on the IC is not restricted to the main line. Below, with freshly painted E6 #4003 in the lead, No. 14, the eastbound *Land o' Corn,* is making a speedy descent into Rockford, Ill., on October 24, 1964. Its westbound counterpart, No. 13, at right, was crossing the Rock River, preparing for the station stop at Rockford a few days before.

At left, with a "frog eyes" Geep rebuilt in the Paducah Shop leading an unmodified and slightly ailing GP9, the "Mendota Turn" local out of Freeport is snarling through Baileyville, Ill., on the old Springfield Division line known as the "Gruber," a name whose origin has been obscured by the years. It's July 1970, and the tall grain elevators stand ready for the harvest season. (BOYD)

One of those grab shots, taken on the spur of the moment but which later becomes an all-time favorite, is this one, above, of a trio of Burlington Fs coming home—rather, passing through their hometown, so to speak—of La Grange, Ill., where they were built many years earlier. The eastbound freight is making a brake reduction on this May 29, 1965, day, running into the yellow of a slower commuter train. Though taken for granted at the time, this picture has since prompted me to paint an O scale model F-unit in this scheme!

How many times have we of the steam-to-diesel transition era read of the local railroad donating "old number such and such" to the citizens of the town. We would read the usual obit of the engine traveling more than a million miles "before today's modern diesel put the noble iron horse out to pasture." We would read vital statistics such as the year it was built, what trains it pulled, and how fast it would go. We would read that the local park was a "permanent place of honor for old such and such" and how this "venerable workhorse would teach the young and remind the old what steam railroading was all about," on *ad nauseam*. Not true in Sterling, Ill.! While it is true that many steam locomotives were sent to scrap at Northwestern Steel & Wire's huge electric furnace at Sterling, NSW's management has seen to it that steam *continues* to switch the huge complex even now as I write this in 1980! The night shot, at lower left, was taken on November 30, 1963, but it could be *tonight!* If you are "of the young who need to be taught," Sterling wouldn't be a bad place to start.

One of the more notable "teachers" of the late 1950s and early '60s was the CB&Q, which was not going to have citizens along its system remember or learn of steam railroading by only presenting cold relics to city parks. The diesel-pioneering railroad saw to it that certain locomotives—most notably 01a Mikado #4960 and 05b Northern #5632 (pictured later in this volume)—be kept in top-notch shape for frequent railfan trips and "choo-choo specials" for school kids. Management—most notably president Harry Murphy—further saw to it that none of the barnstorming steamers was artificially dolled up in the usual "white-walled tire, white-trim attire," but remained painted as it was in service: tasteful. The 4960 is pictured at upper right heading west near Sandwich, Ill., on a beautifully cold, crisp December 19, 1965.

Below, a Chinese red GP7, renumbered for the recent Burlington Northern merger, punctuates the lull between commuter trains, speeding east through La Grange on November 4, 1971. (*NSW*, BOYD; *all others*, BALL)

The Illinois Terminal Company originally entered Peoria on its interurban right of way that traversed city streets and went up and down hills and around curves that were fine for a trolley car but were quite an operating problem for freight trains. With the demise of its passenger business in the 1950s, the ITC began concentrating on its role as a freight hauler between Peoria, Springfield, and St. Louis. To gain an easier climb out of the Illinois River valley, the ITC acquired trackage rights over a branch of the Pennsylvania R.R. Above, the afternoon freight into Peoria is making its way over weed-crowded rails at Morton, Ill., on a bright July day in 1966. The motive power is three GP7s with an SW1200 tucked in as the third unit.

At left, adorned in different shades of green and yellow, Toledo, Peoria & Western RS2 #203 is working the west yard lead of the road's home terminal in East Peoria in 1964. In addition to serving the local communities on its line, the TP&W is an important short cut between the Santa Fe at the Mississippi River and the Pennsylvania R.R. at the Illinois-Indiana state line.

Above right, another variation on the green theme is the handsome Chicago & Illinois Midland. While it does handle some merchandise and agricultural traffic—as evidenced by the Pillsbury flour mill that forms the backdrop for the Midland's Springfield, Ill., yard—the C&IM's primary traffic is coal, most of it bound for owner Commonwealth Edison's power plants in Chicago and northern Illinois. The C&IM owns only 18 diesels, and at least one of each of its four types is represented at Springfield on this June day in 1965: SW1200 #18, SD9s #52 and #54, RS1325 #31—one of only two in existence—and SD18 #61, the trailing unit.

One never appreciates how perfectly EMD handled the esthetics of its F units until one sees what happens when the Silvis shops removes the top headlight on the nose, as was done with Rock Island F2 #49, at right, leading a westbound manifest through Wyanet, Ill., in October 1966. (*ITC*, BALL; *all other*, BOYD)

The true second-generation train of the 60s and 70s is the unit train, operating as a complete, captive, never-to-be-broken-up consist between two points; a conveyer belt that loads and unloads, always on the move. The first such train "in the flesh" in my railroad journey was Commonwealth Edison's unit train between the mine at Percy, in southern Illinois, and the generating plant at Plains, just below Joliet. Each afternoon, four or five flashy "Big Red" SD40s would couple on to the 125 Thrall-built 100-ton hoppers and head south. Once under way, it was a great train to chase

and pace by car. A most enjoyable experience for me—really a thrill—was to stand at trackside and feel this train hammer past. *Clickety-clack, clickety-clack, clickety-clack*—an almost endless, repetitious conveyor belt of identical cars drumming over the rails, fanning up a breeze in their wake. Fun!

Above, 12,000 horsepower worth of SD40s back down to knuckle onto their Commonwealth Edison train at Plains on Memorial Day 1964. (BALL)

5

WE CAN HANDLE IT

AMERICAN FREEDOM TRAIN FOUNDATION
AMTRAK
ATCHISON, TOPEKA AND SANTA FE RAILWAY CO.
BLACK MESA & LAKE POWELL RAILROAD
BURLINGTON NORTHERN INC.
CANADIAN NATIONAL RAILWAY
CANADIAN PACIFIC
CHICAGO, BURLINGTON & QUINCY RAILROAD
CHICAGO, MILWAUKEE, ST. PAUL AND PACIFIC RAILROAD CO.
CHICAGO, ROCK ISLAND AND PACIFIC RAILROAD CO.
COLORADO AND SOUTHERN RAILWAY CO.
DENVER & RIO GRANDE WESTERN RAILROAD CO.
GULF, MOBILE AND OHIO RAILROAD
KANSAS CITY, KAW VALLEY RAILROAD
KANSAS CITY SOUTHERN LINES
LOUISIANA & NORTH WEST RAILROAD
MAGMA ARIZONA RAILROAD
MISSOURI-KANSAS-TEXAS RAILROAD CO.
MISSOURI PACIFIC RAILROAD CO.
NATIONAL RAILWAYS OF MEXICO
ST. LOUIS-SAN FRANCISCO RAILWAY CO.
ST. LOUIS SOUTHWESTERN RAILWAY CO.
SPOKANE, PORTLAND AND SEATTLE RAILWAY SYSTEM
SOUTHERN PACIFIC LINES
TEXAS AND PACIFIC RAILWAY (610 FOUNDATION)
UNION PACIFIC RAILROAD
UNITED STATES STEEL CORP.
UTAH RAILWAY CO.
WESTERN PACIFIC RAILROAD CO.

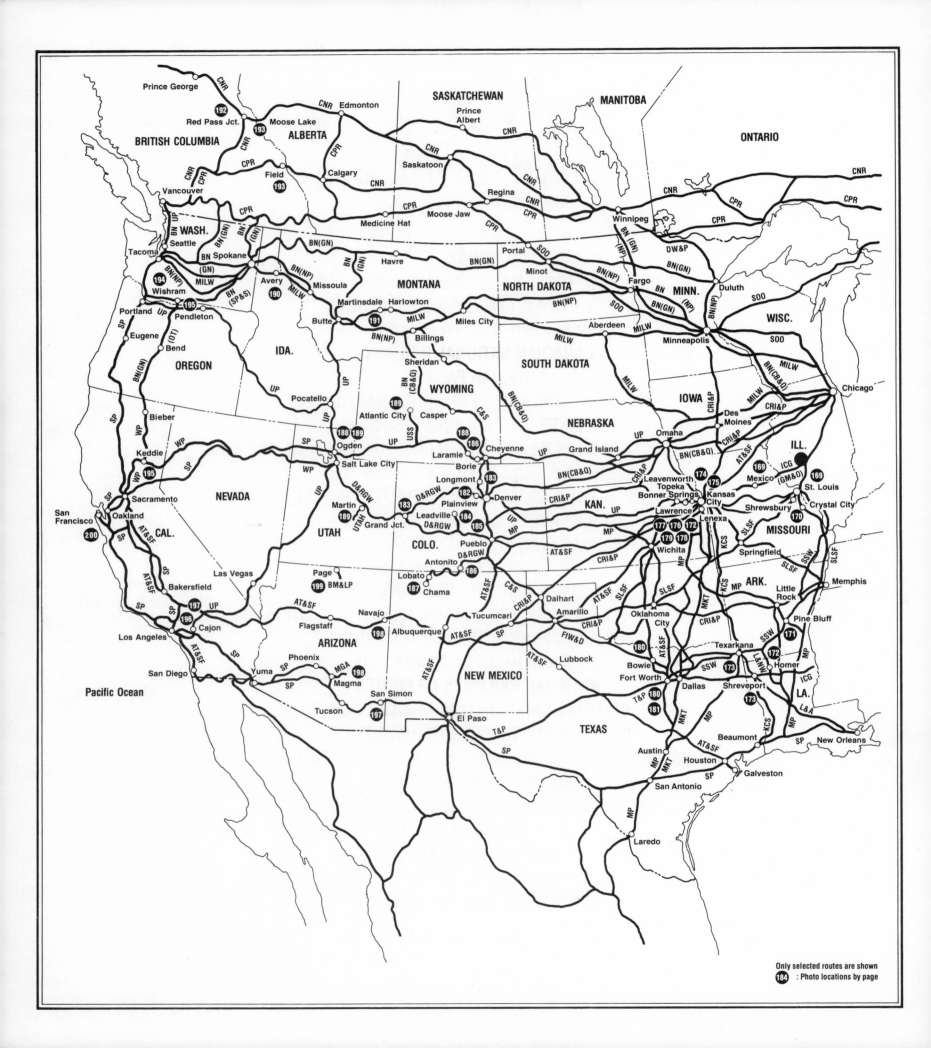

Only selected routes are shown

(184) : Photo locations by page

MY WIFE couldn't believe I was heading over to Bonner Springs for "another day of trains." This was the second day of our visit with her folks in Prairie Village and, yes, I did realize I was playing a little game of "in-law brinkmanship" by being away on the second day of our visit. I would probably try for the third, too, and, perhaps, the fourth, but that would require some crafty thinking—or guts!

Bonner Springs, Kansas, is on a bend on the Kaw River, exactly 17.5 miles west of Kansas City's Union Station. It is hilly for Kansas and just about the last place in the state where groves of oak trees give way to the open country as you head west. Bonner Springs was always the place I journeyed east to from Lawrence for scenic photography—and to enjoy the countryside itself. I have always preferred the hilly country just west of Bonner Springs toward Loring, where the Union Pacific climbs upgrade from river's edge.

Bonner Springs is a place where I have found only very simple things to enjoy. There is a certain remoteness from urban confusion in the town, and while this sense of peace can be found in other places, Bonner Springs offers it unpretentiously with such grace—and familiarity—that no other place will suffice for me. The immediate countryside has changed little since I was a boy, and it seems to satisfy something in me that has gone hungry since childhood. It's difficult to put this feeling in writing. Bonner Springs is simply a place to listen to the rustle of oak leaves in the breeze, the nail-driving call of ringnecks down by the river, and the shrill whistle of bobwhite quail. It is an area whose gentle, natural sounds seem as old as life itself. With the exception of the welded rail—and, of course, the motive power and rolling stock—the railroad looks very much the same.

There is history, fascinating history, in this largely unchanged land, too— history that, for the most part, has gone unnoticed. Sometime around 1566, Coronado and his exploration party were supposed to have set up camp near here for the winter. Legend has it that Bonner Springs was the fabled Quivira with golden streets. While Coronado found no evidence of gold in the area, evidence of his presence exists. Spanish halberds dating back to the 1500s have been found in the region. In early American history, the area was known as Coronado Springs, where early conquistadors bathed and were refreshed. The most common historic name for Bonner Springs is Tiblow. This name may have come from a club-footed Indian named Henry Tiblow, who supposedly operated a ferry across the Kaw River in the mid-1800s. On the other hand, Henry Tiblow may have adopted this "un-Indian" name from the town since Tiblow means houses or settlement, and four substantial cabins were built here between 1812 and 1821 by Francis and Cyprian Chouteau, French traders. Records also indicate that Tiblow was renamed Tiblow Trading Post shortly before the Kansas Pacific Railroad came through along the north bank of the Kaw on its far-flung endeavor to reach the West Coast. A little trivia about a favorite place.

Way up in the sky a silver jet leaves a contrail behind on its transcontinental journey. A chainsaw can be heard occasionally. I quickly realize that the most commonplace sights and sounds of a few decades ago are either going or have already gone. The soft music of the land and the comfort of its gentle sounds are, to me, most precious resources. Way off I hear one of the most distinctive and appealing sounds in nature—the resonant and sonorous "uh-Whonk, uh-Whonk" of Canadian geese on the move. Their call is close now. The wavy, constantly undulating dark lines of geese appear overhead in erratic V formations, dissolving and forming, heading north. Spring has come again to the land.

In this volume I'm concerned with Bonner Spring's history *after* 1960. During this time, there were many changes in the railroad scene at Bonner Springs, one of the most profound of which was the loss of the tower, known as BW, that guarded the crossing of the Union Pacific and Santa Fe. Why, BW's operators John Gallahue and L. O. Shamblin were always glad to offer shade in their tower on a 100-degree day, and they always knew when and from where the next train would be coming. Windows opened up east and west and south toward the river, and I'm sure the temperature inside was always 20 degrees cooler. In November 1961, the neat three-story tower was ground up into brick rubble and replaced by electronic equipment.

As if the loss of the tower was not a big enough change (mind you, the "unchanged area" I'm talking about is just a small area west of town), the Kansas City Kaw Valley Railroad formally announced total abandonment of operations with its last run scheduled for December 28, 1961. This would end 51 years of interurban operations out of Bonner Springs. The right of way would then be used to widen K-32 highway into a modern four-lane affair along the Kaw from the east.

Work on the Kansas City & Bonner Springs Electric Line was started in 1904, and a year later, after a lapse in construction progress, a politically and financially stronger Kansas City Western Railroad emerged with the ultimate goal of reaching westward into Bonner Springs from Kansas City and on to Lawrence and Topeka. The Missouri & Kansas Interurban Railway and the Kansas City & Olathe Railway got into the act, both announcing Lawrence and Topeka as westward goals. In March 1908, the Kansas City & Bonner Springs Electric Line elected new officers and started to build its railroad. In June 1909, the company was officially chartered as the Kansas City Kaw Valley Railroad. More funding brought more changes and on Monday, July 20, 1917, the Kansas City, Kaw Valley & Western Railroad began operations between Kansas City, Kans., Bonner Springs, and Lawrence. On December 1, 1949, the 22-mile segment from Bonner Springs to Lawrence was abandoned, but after that, the little railroad remained a "permanent fixture" around Bonner Springs. Most of the business came from the Lone Star Cement plant east of Bonner and the Safeway Cereal plant and Lauhoff Grain Company plant, both behind BW tower; all three concerns providing ample carloads to keep the three yellow 50-ton Baldwin-Westinghouse steeple-cab locomotives on the run.

The abnormal quiet along the Union Pacific prompts me to drive back toward town to Union Pacific's corrugated steel building. This building replaced the recently demolished white clapboard station (another change). Inside, the agent-operator checks with the dispatcher and gives me the lineup for both Union Pacific and Rock Island trains. The unusual lull in traffic gives me plenty of time to get over to Lawrence.

My fondest diesel experience—I should say second-generation diesel experience—took place in Lawrence in the spring of 1965. I had been away for a few years, and it was time to go back and renew acquaintances in the UP depot. I naturally did not expect much in the way of trains since a yellow diesel is a yellow diesel and I didn't like diesels. Besides, by 1964 I had established myself as a fairly good freight-car peddler, so my interests naturally leaned toward what was being pulled and not what was pulling. I had even shelved my cameras, for the most part, with the demise of main-line steam in 1960 and had reverted my railroad-hobby interests to "modeling memories" in the basement. I drove up beside the depot and headed for the agent's door. Down toward the massive co-op grain elevators, a yellow Geep switched covered hoppers, scattering the pilfering pigeons into flight. John Robinson, who had been the telegrapher during my youth and was now the agent, greeted me with a "Well, where have you been ol' buddy?" I felt at home.

As with railcars, technology had changed the ways of the UP depot since I was last there. One gadget that immediately catches my eye is the hot-box detector unit between the windows that face the tracks. Coming from the west, trains pass the scanner located out toward Buck Creek, and the heat given off by each journal is translated into electric impulses that cause a marking needle to jump on the rotating drum of paper, much as a seismograph does when registering the earth's tremors. If the needle *really* jumps, you know you've got a hot box! Long sections of marked paper from trains that have gone by earlier in the day lie in the wastepaper basket. Each train is a long series of short horizontal lines marked left to right, top to bottom, with car lengths being the only variant in spacing between the parallel lines. If there is a hot or warm journal, the agent watching the graph can quickly see where the trouble is in the train. John explains that just west of the curve there is a hold signal that is red at all times. Once the train passes the scanner and the "tape is good," he then manually clears the hold signal and the train continues. If there is a problem, the hold stays red, the train stops, and its crew is notified on the radio of the approximate car in question. Westbound trains hit the scanner at the Eudora crossing east of town.

An amber light flicks on over the machine, indicating an approaching eastbound. In seconds, the revolving drum starts and we watch the needle. Three hash marks, a space, three hash marks repeated four more times, indicates five six-motored diesels are on the point. The needle "double-jumps" for each car's wheels and it's easy to differentiate immediately between the 40' cars and the 57' cars—and especially the 89' cars. This train has lots of the 89' cars, most likely auto racks and piggyback flats. The caboose shows up as four marks closely spaced, and the train is "all black," meaning nothing hot. The hold is cleared. The throbbing engines approach and roar on past. Watching the passing cars, I feel as though I've seen this train somewhere before!

UP seems to like bunching up trains. I always remember that when I see one train, there will be more. Sure enough, the light is back on over the machine and we have another eastbound. "This time you watch," John says. The machine is activated and immediately the needle jumps four times, four times again; four times, four times again—then resumes the normal double skips for each wheel set. I quickly alert John to the needle's odd behavior and he joins me. "Looks like two choppers on this one." I'm baffled by his remark. "Haven't you seen our 31-class engines?" John asks. I obviously don't know what a 31-class engine is. John clears the hold and we go out on the platform, reminiscent of steam days when I would run out onto the platform and wait to see what engine would round the curve. But this is 1965, so I'm not expecting to see steam! In fact, I'm being polite, not expecting to see much of anything. Now I hear it—*this* train is making a lot of noise and it sounds different. There is a thunderous chanting whine and an increasingly loud, syncopating, pulsing *blat-blat-blat-blat* of the damnedest sounding machinery. A towering bus-looking creature, articulating on span-bolster trucks, looms up on the curve with a mate, sending smoke swirling into the air—the fierce rage of noise testifying to its power—sounding as if it will tear itself apart. The ground actually tremors when both of the multiple-wheeled monsters blat on past, reminding me of steam's way of shaking things. The engines tower over the large cars behind, and I am really taken! In a crazy way, Union Pacific's big 9000s have come back.

The 31-class engines I saw that day were a pair of new GE U50s developing

10,000 horsepower and weighing over a million pounds. They brought me back to Lawrence and Bonner—cameras and all—on the run!

Throughout the following years, I have been back at trackside along the UP, and, yes, I had a love affair with the big U50s and the newer U50Cs that followed. John Robinson retired in 1965, and Roy Dent replaced him. Ken Bauman came over to Lawrence in August 1971 and is still there. Another "gadget" came to Lawrence, too— the ASR-35 teletype that constantly prints out manifests of all UP trains well in advance of their estimated time. The hot-box detector and its accompanying hold signals are now controlled by the dispatcher, and sadly, incredibly, the big U50s and U50Cs are gone—ironically, victims of the increasingly standardized and lighter second-generation diesels that can be accommodated on run-through trains off the UP property. As I write this, the '70s are coming to a close, and it looks like the changes around Lawrence are not going to let up. The Rock Island is bankrupt and facing outright extinction. The Union Pacific is on the verge of rapid expansion and could become our nation's first really transcontinental railroad. I suspect the Santa Fe will always come through Lawrence, but I wonder what other roads will become a part of Santa Fe's trail?

No doubt about it, the fascination with railroads and railroading will continue, with change at the throttle, keeping us at trackside. Consider, if you will, that something as incredibly massive and modern as a U50C can become extinct overnight, while something as fragile as Union Pacific's yellow coat of paint can last for decades. I don't think we can afford to turn our backs on trains and railroading . . . today will never be the same.

A word or two about the ex–Texas & Pacific Texas type #610 that pulled the American Freedom Train in Texas. I made the decision not to get into the building of the AFT in this book, but I've got to at least mention the 610 and get some of this story out of my heart and onto these pages. Those close to the inner circle of people charged with getting the Train designed, built, and on the rails know I tried to keep personal emotions and desires to myself when we were checking steam locomotive "candidates" around the country for possible restoration to pull the AFT. I periodically called David Morgan at TRAINS for his thoughts and advice, and to appraise him of what the "current thinking" was, but other than that, not much was said outside the foundation headquarters. Texas & Pacific #610 was the exception to this self-imposed rule for many irresistible reasons. For one thing, the T&P 600-class was the most notable exception to my fairly comprehensive life-time log of steam locomotives seen in service, a fact I had been sorely aware of ever since reading about T&P's #638 being presented to the Texas State Fair in Dallas on December 22, 1949, wrapped with a giant ribbon and billed as the "world's biggest Christmas gift." Incredibly, the 638 was left alone and without a fence (can I say defenceless?) at the fairgrounds, and vandals did their thing over the next five years. In the spring of 1955, the now-turned-eyesore #638 was scrapped on the spot. The loss was tragic. Over the next several years, rumors persisted that another 600-class Texas type had escaped the scrapper's torch, but this could not be verified.

More than 10 years later on a business trip through Texas, I found the rumor to be incredibly true—the 610 had indeed been saved, her fate seemingly known only to local residents around Fort Worth. I later contacted the owner and made up my mind that *somehow* she would run again.

Now, #610 is not just another run-of-the-erecting-shop steam locomotive; she is the genuine Lima Super-Power article from 1927. In 1925, Lima introduced Super-Power to the railroads in the form of 2-8-4 Berkshire No. 1. This locomotive was a huge (for the era), high-horsepower machine that changed operating-department philosophies overnight, offering for the first time superior starting tractive effort and near–passenger-train performance on freight. Possessing a large firebox riding on a 4-wheel supporting truck, a big boiler with higher pressure, booster engine, and feedwater superheater, No. 1 had the horsepower to pull and run like no other steam locomotive had ever run before. She was brute power and speed. She would influence every steam locomotive designed from that point on. The Texas & Pacific loved the barnstorming 2-8-4, and, as Texans so often do, the T&P ordered a "large version" with two more driving wheels to support the bigger boiler. The first 2-10-4, #600, was delivered to the Texas & Pacific one year after No. 1 made its successful debut. #610 arrived on the property in 1927.

During World War II, I kept a large scrapbook that I filled with magazine and newspaper pictures of America's railroads on the home front. One of my favorite pictures was an ad that showed a big Texas & Pacific 600 on an oil train "Defeating Hitler's Wolf Pack." The photograph was backlit, accentuating the bulk and fearsome-looking, pipe-laden engine—all in all the perfect scrapbook locomotive. Friend Joe Collias talked of the 600's "most pleasingly impressive head-end countenance"; David Morgan may have summed it all up in a phone conversation when he said: "The 610 certainly has the man-appeal you want in a big steam locomotive."

Scrapbook dreams became tangible ones with the chance of using #610 on the American Freedom Train. Locomotive mechanic Dick Jensen was hired to start restoration of the 610, and Amon G. Carter, Jr., publisher of the *Fort Worth Star Telegram*, provided the needed publicity—and a matching dollar for every dollar donated—to assure a chance of success. Restoration progress was discussed by phone almost on a daily basis. On January 28, 1976, my scrapbook dream became a reality when a fire was lit and water was poured into 610's boiler. We didn't get off the engine that bright Wednesday until around 4:00 P.M. when the steam gauges indicated she was ready to move! After 26 years, #610 moved under her own steam—the first "destination" being several hundred feet backward to a clear spot so I could take some rodsdown pictures of her under a blue Texas sky—and under the squirrel's tail of her very own pops. The total impression of 610 was everything I had dreamed it would be. Even more beautiful—her being alive was the fulfillment of a dream, an achievement worth cheering tomorrow and building on thereafter. The full story will certainly be told some day.

In *America's Colorful Railroads,* I talked about and illustrated what I believed was "perhaps America's most colorful railroad." I was referring, of course, to the Gulf, Mobile & Ohio and its red, maroon, and gold paint scheme that was a derivative of the famous "red train," the *Alton Limited* of 1899! The fact that the paint scheme was surviving into the '40s and '50s was quite amazing.

Now, we're talking the '60s and '70s, and here is the Gulf, Mobile & Ohio still with us in that same red, maroon, and gold! The little two-car train pictured at upper right is GM&O's No. 10 at Mexico, Mo. on April 4, 1960. The fact that this 1928-vintage gas-electric train (known more affectionately as a "doodlebug") survived into the '60s is in itself quite amazing. This throwback to prediesel railroading meandered through 362 miles of countryside between Bloomington, Ill., and Kansas City *each day,* making an incredible 60 stops! Sadly, 10 days after this picture was taken, the little train was finally discontinued.

At lower right, in March of 1970, Gulf, Mobile & Ohio's train No. 2, the *Abraham Lincoln,* makes its 8:58 departure out of St. Louis en route to Chicago. History rode the beautiful train until May 1, 1971, when Amtrak took over. (BALL, BOYD)

Mention the railroad names St. Louis–San Francisco or St. Louis Southwestern to any but the most seasoned railfan and you'll likely get a moment of puzzled contemplation before their more familiar names pop into mind: the Frisco and the Cotton Belt. Although similar in formal names, the two are as different as their nicknames. The Frisco, which laces Missouri and Oklahoma like a steel octopus, is a fiercely competitive independent carrier, while the Cotton Belt, which departs St. Louis and heads directly for Arkansas and Texas, is a subsidiary of the Southern Pacific and provides that western giant with its most important eastern connection.

The Cotton Belt indulged in only minimal passenger service—it never owned more than four passenger diesels in its entire history—while the Frisco ran a proud fleet covering almost its entire system with trains ranging from elegant streamliners to folksy accommodations with mail cars and an old arch-roof coach. An example of the latter is the Memphis–St. Louis segment of the *Sunnyland*; above left, train No. 808 was northbound on the River Division at

Crystal City, Mo., in early September 1965 behind E8 #2011 in the newer spartanized paint scheme. Like #2012, below left, the 2011 had previously borne the name of a famous racehorse, in its case, *Gallant Fox*. Breezing through Shrewsbury, Mo., in June 1965 on the *Meteor*, the overnight pride of the fleet between St. Louis and Oklahoma City, the 2012 was living up to its *Flying Ebony* name. No name, however, was more appropriate for a Frisco E8 than the one emblazoned on the scarlet flanks of #2020: *Big Red*.

Above, bearing down on Rone Siding at a mile a minute, the MBSM—*Memphis Blue Streak Merchandise*—has a brand new Southern Pacific SD45 leading a mix of Cotton Belt and SP units in May 1968. All three modern locomotive builders are represented in the consist, with the EMD SD45 and two F7s, an Alco RS11 and a GE U25B. Temporarily off his regular job on the Little Rock branch local, engineer John Page really has 'em rolling down the Cotton Belt main line a few miles out of Pine Bluff, Ark., bound for Texarkana. (BOYD)

171

At left, the newest diesels on the railroad, SD40-2s #602 and #607, are rolling a Missouri-Kansas-Texas freight into the evening sun at Lenexa, Kan., on January 4, 1969. The "Katy" is running here on Frisco track, which it uses for the first 42 miles out of Kansas City.

Although its back-to-back F7s have the style of a main-line railroad, below, the Louisiana & North West is a 61-mile short line in south central Arkansas and northern Louisiana. In the late-afternoon light of November 1969, the two units are northbound above Homer, La., headed for the Cotton Belt connection at McNeil, Ark., with a trainload of paper products brought up from the mill in Hodge, La., by another short line, the North Louisiana & Gulf.

They called 'em "ghosts," when the new SD40s introduced the solid-white paint scheme to the formerly red-and-yellow Kansas City Southern in 1966. At right, three of the big white ghosts are working a southbound freight into Texarkana in April 1969. A month later, below right, a mix of older KCS power is seen working another southbound freight through the streets of Shreveport, La. The lead F3 is one of the few remaining "blondes" with the yellow window band; more typical is the solid red on the F7B and two trailing GP30s. That's the Shreveport Union Station at the extreme right. (*MKT;* BALL; *all others,* BOYD)

By the early '60s many of the railroads were letting their once prestigious passenger trains dwindle down to basic conveyances, and it was often a case of adding insult to injury by keeping the once proud train name on the remnants. Sad sight it is, watching what's left of Missouri Pacific's *Missouri River Eagle* drifting to a station stop at Leavenworth, Kans., above, on July 27, 1962. Although this scene has always been, at best, a melancholy one to me, Jim was absolutely ecstatic at the sight of an MP PA3, especially in the original colors; what was depressingly commonplace in Kansas in 1962 has become a treasure in 1980. At lower left, we're standing on Union Pacific's eastbound track in Bonner Springs, Kans., watching Kansas City Kaw Valley's freight motors exiting their barn for a day's work; the date is March 3, 1961. Their permanent exit is not far away. At upper right, an eastbound Rock Island hotshot approaches Bonner Springs on January 2, 1973, with minimally relettered former UP F9 units leading the parade. Below right, wouldn't you like to see the box that engine came in? Looking like the world's grandest brass model, Burlington's famed Northern #5632 heads toward Kansas City Union Station on May 20, 1964, to pick up the Golden Anniversary Special commemorating 50 years of train service in and out of Union Station. (BALL)

To the west, the sun sends blades of orange and gold between the few wispy clouds low on the horizon. The tremendous sky is clear everywhere else, and now, with the red ball sitting right on the horizon, the eastern sky starts to lose light. Darkness falls onto the ground and the remaining sunlight goes warm rose. Both eastbound and westbound approach lights blink green and we have two trains. The light is fast fading. Two headlights appear across the distant land, and, as luck would have it, the westbound is moving decidedly faster—decidedly like a bat! Rock Island's evening hotshot to Houston is overdue, and the white, blue, yellow, red, and maroon units are easily discernible,

approaching across the flat country. No. 28 is flying! She's frozen forever, above, on the Midland, Kans., curve on January 3, 1979. At upper right earlier the same day, and at the urging of my son, "Take a picture, Dad!" we pan the Rock Island GP38-2 handling the 41-car train known as "01" west of Lawrence. The practice of letting a Rock train out on the main with only a single diesel drives multiple-unit-minded UP dispatchers nuts! At lower right, and taken the previous day when the prairie grasses were ablaze, UP's symbol OKS fans the smoldering embers, heading east toward Lawrence and Kansas City. My son, Fenner, looks on. (BALL)

Uncle Pete! In second-generation diesels, nothing was more impressive! In the nineteenth century, the Union Pacific's wailing whistles spoke of muscle, money, and romance. In the first half of the twentieth century the thundering steam locomotives spoke of adventure made real. Today, Union Pacific dramatically remains the very symbol of conquest with its massive power and frequent trains. Above, the second section of KNP hits the Midland curve on December 28, 1973, with its monstrous U50 dwarfing the otherwise large units behind. At left, U50C #5033 towers high, heading the westbound *Omaha Express* (OEX) out of Lawrence, Kans., on August 9, 1976. At upper right, and closing in at over 80 mph, U50C #5014 leads symbol OKC, meeting westbound AKO (*Advance Kansas Omaha*) with the 5033, again, on the curve in Lawrence on August 11, 1976. At right, and caught in the last seconds of direct sun, #3046 leads two EMDs and the AKO between the massive coop grain elevators in Lawrence, westbound on January 4, 1976. The 3046, I discover later, is a rare SD40X, former EMD test locomotive 434G, one of the first units to carry EMD's 645 diesel engine, the standard for the next decade. (BALL)

Throughout the whole planning and execution phases of the American Freedom Train project, only once did I place personal interest first, and that was with the ex–Texas & Pacific 2-10-4 #610—an engine I never saw in regular service but always wished I had. All past problems and apprehensions were quickly laid to rest when, after 26 years of sleep, we moved #610 back for her first rods-down portrait under a full head of steam in Ft. Worth on January 28, 1976. Glorious! Below, she's at full stride on her first test run, passing through Bowie, Texas, on February 4.

At right, an inbound Rock Island freight behind new reds and old maroons heads toward its Peach Street Yard destination as a Ft. Worth & Denver freight departs. In an era when *any* wood caboose is a rarity, consider the irony of an outside-braced gem in the fresh colors of a space-age corporate image bringing up the markers—oops, no marker— of an outbound manifest. The location is in the Trinity Valley just west of Ft. Worth. At lower right, five minutes later and on the other side of the bridge, Amtrak's *Lone Star* heads out of town on Santa Fe iron behind SDP40s. The date for both pictures is February 2, 1976. (BAL

The $27 shot. The picture at left may very well be the "most perfect photograph" in this whole book—and it was a grab shot! I'll explain. T.J. was en route to Oakland, via Amtrak, in February 1974 and stopped off at Denver to ride the *Rio Grande Zephyr,* allowing an afternoon for photography. He rented a car from Hertz, found Route 72 and headed for Rio Grande's Tunnel No. 1 on the Front Range. No sooner had he reached the railroad and parked the car when he heard the throbbing turbochargers of a westbound train approaching on the loop below. Not used to high altitude and deep snow, T.J. bounded for his desired tunnel-top location. But didn't make it! The rapidly ascending freight thundered over the highway in Coal Creek Canyon and scaled the mountainside toward the tunnel. Wheeling around and shooting by instinct, T.J. nailed his "grab" shot. It was the only thing he had to show for the $27 car rental, and it wasn't until he had the film developed that he discovered that his "failure" wasn't one after all. At right, and another encounter between T.J. and the Rio Grande, the *California Zephyr* is pictured at Grand Junction, Col., five hours after it had arrived. A huge thunderstorm threatened mud and rock slides up ahead, so the train "waited it out" in a manner more typical of an airliner. When it was time to depart, the engineer blew the horn for ten minutes, emptying the movie theater, shops, and restaurants! Temperature on this October 1962 day was in the 90s but dropped into the 50s as the gigantic storm moved east. Below, it's the Fourth of July 1969 as a Colorado & Southern freight rolls northward through the high country near Longmont, Col. Although its locomotives wear the Chinese red of parent CB&Q, the C&S retains its corporate identity and operates as a separate railroad. Motive power on this Denver to Cheyenne train consists of a C&S U30C, CB&Q GP40 and a C&S SD40. (DONAHUE, DONAHUE, BOYD)

Leadville, Colorado. Land of legends and silver-rich lead ores, a booming land of over 30,000 people—mostly miners —by 1880. Denver & Rio Grande's narrow gauge rails arrived in town that year from Cañon City, 116 miles away. The Denver, South Park & Pacific came to town, too, but over the rails of the D&RG for the last 40 miles. In 1883, a dispute brought an end to this "40-mile friendship," and the South Park spiked track up over the 11,330-foot Fremont Pass from Dickey, becoming the only railroad in Colorado to build eastward across the Continental Divide. Through mergers and takeovers, segments of the legendary South Park became part of the Colorado & Southern, Burlington and, ultimately, Burlington Northern. In June 1943, the last remnant of the narrow-gauge empire was replaced by standard gauge, and this remains today the highest regular railroad line in the U.S. Now isolated from the rest of the C&S/BN system, the Leadville Branch has been operated by

one locomotive at a time for most of its modern history. The resident C&S 2-8-0 #641 worked into the early 1960s, as witness its leaving town belching a fine plume of smoke—in answer to the photographer's request—on May 5, 1962. Once offered to the D&RGW, which turned it down, the line grew extremely profitable for the C&S with technology's finding more and more uses for the products of the molybdenum mine at Climax. The 2-8-0 was retired to a park near the depot and replaced by SD9 #828, which still uses the venerable engine house which was the home of #641. At upper right, #828 is seen leaving town in August 1977 with the engine house in view. At right, Rio Grande's Pueblo to Minturn local gets out of town several hours behind schedule, that same day, putting in a rare appearance in daylight hours. If there are mountain lovers in the audience, that's Mt. Elbert, highest peak in the Rockies, in the background in both the C&S and BN shots. (BALL, BOYD, BOYD)

Now, here's a spread for the author! No man-made contrivance has ever captured the heart and soul as has the steam locomotive—and all the reasons why have been written a thousand eloquent ways. Those of us who grew up with steam and got it in our blood will gladly travel a thousand miles to see a live steamer—as many of us have done to see Union Pacific's and Rio Grande's sole survivors. Union Pacific's mighty symbol of steam, FEF-3 class 4-8-4 #8444, is pictured at left, charging through a Wyoming blizzard down off of Sherman Hill, heading east near Borie on February 20, 1971. At right, and in the stillness of a lovely Indian summer day in October 1960, Rio Grande's 2-8-2 #484 speaks to the heavens, blasting northward toward Lobatto trestle in New Mexico. In the distance, Windy Point. Below, we pace a northbound D&RGW narrow-gauge train near Romeo, N. Mex., on June 3, 1960—both the train and ourselves outpacing a vicious thunderstorm. (BALL, BALL, DONAHUE)

Once again, the story is Union Pacific and its insatiable thirst for motive power. The railroad that had the largest rigid-wheelbase steam locomotive and the biggest-in-the-world articulateds opted for the most-powerful-in-the-world 8,500-horsepower gas turbine locomotives from General Electric. Diesels got in the act, too, with all three U.S. builders delivering the world's most powerful diesels built especially for Union Pacific. Above, and that's well over 20,000 yellow UP horsepower on the point, one of the huge turbines, now upgraded to a whopping 10,000 h.p., seemingly blows defiance at the smaller big diesels behind, heading the entourage of power, and a train, eastbound through Weber Canyon, Utah, in July 1969. Moments later, the road's first largest-in-the-world Centennial diesel headed west, at upper right, with the majestic Wasatch forming the backdrop. At left, Alco's entry into the double-engined diesels, the Century 855,

snorts like a pack of angry RS1s getting a westbound into Laramie, Wyo., on August 27, 1965. The single unit is delivering 5,500 h.p.—more than a first-generation 4-unit FT diesel! My first impression of the beast was a bloodhound; the name that came to mind—Throgmorton. At middle right, two Utah Railway RSD4s head toward Martin, Utah, on April 23, 1965, with black diamonds out of Mohrland. This all-Alco railroad is the favorite for those of us longing for some Alco-produced reverie. At lower right, ex–B&LE F7s and a lone UP unit prepare to leave Atlantic City, Wyo., with iron-ore pellets bound for parent U.S. Steel's plant at Geneva, Utah, on a beautiful June 1966 day. (BOYD, BALL, BOYD, BALL, COLLECTION)

Climbing westward toward St. Paul Pass in Idaho's Bitter Root Mountains, Milwaukee Road "Little Joe" E79, above, is actually leading eastbound hotshot 262, the *Thunderhawk,* out of the valley of the North Fork of the St. Joe River in July 1969. Built by GE in 1948 for Soviet Russia, this 273-ton locomotive was embargoed by the cold war and sold as one of 12 to the Milwaukee in 1950. At right, dropping down from the crest at Loweth, Mont., the E76 is working in multiple with an SD45 and GP40s on the *Thunderhawk* in October 1971 approaching Martinsdale. The crystal-clear air and autumn colors etched an almost surrealistic landscape.

The original motive power on the Milwaukee's electrification was a fleet of massive GE boxcabs built in 1915–1916. Using a 3,000-volt DC system, they were the marvels of their age. An even greater marvel is that they were still running in October 1971, departing Avery, Idaho, at left, and heading up the canyon of the North Fork of the St. Joe with hotshot freight 264. With the E34B leading the three-unit road power, No. 264 this day has a four-unit set of mid-train helpers led by the E50A, the former 10200A, the first Milwaukee freight electric delivered in 1915! (BOYD)

In the 1880s, men struggling with the bitterest of Mother Nature's elements got the Canadian Pacific over the continental divide through Kicking Horse Pass, while it wasn't until 1914 that rival Canadian National traversed the divide through Yellowhead Pass, well to the north. Both railroads are pictured, surrounded by scenery known by few people. At far left, the wildflowers usher in spring as a varied lashup of CN diesels lead a westbound west of Red Pass Jct., Alta. Those extra lights on the SD40 are ditch lights—on for obvious reasons! At left, CN's *Super Continental* is pictured eastbound at Moose Lake. Moments after it passed, it snowed. All of these photos, I might add, were taken in late June 1976. Below, two Canadian Pacific F-units painted in the road's Action Red colors, lead the beautiful *Canadian* up through Kicking Horse Valley over the Otter Tail River, six miles west of Field, Alta. In a few minutes, the dome riders in the "Skyline Coffee Shop" and "Algonquin Park" Observation will have the complete President Range in view, from Emerald Lake to the lofty peaks of President, Mount Burgess and Mount Carnarvon, Mounts Cathedral and Stephen—scenery that travelers on board the *Canadian* are crossing the continent to look at. (DONAHUE)

Never in the odyssey of American Freedom Train's ex–Southern Pacific Daylight was a day more beautiful for *The Queen* than on May 12, 1975, when she got out on the Burlington Northern's SP&S main line with a revenue freight from Vancouver to Wishram, Wash. At left, hold on! Extra 4449 West has departed Wishram on the fast return run and has the high cars rolling! How quickly 16 years of sleep in Portland's Oak Park, and six months of dedicated restoration—let alone the months of hassling to obtain her—were forgotten! At lower left, a somewhat less spectacular BN freight behind an SD45 is pictured, same place, same unbelievable day! At right, and in the days before Burlington Northern, a Spokane, Portland & Seattle freight heads east along the Columbia River on June 28, 1965, behind the typical Alco lashup that endeared the railroad to diesel railfans: two C424s, FA1s, and an RS3. Below, a Western Pacific westbound from Salt Lake City to Oakland spans the famous Keddie Wye at Keddie, Calif., seconds before plunging into a tunnel in July 1968. Note the steam-styled headlights on the lead GP35. (*W.P.,* BOYD; *all others,* BALL)

Cajon Pass, the mountain gateway to the Los Angeles basin, is conquered by the rails of the Santa Fe, Union Pacific and Southern Pacific. At left, in March 1975, the Santa Fe is using its premier *Super C* piggyback train to introduce its first locomotive repainted for the Bicentennial. SD45-2 #5700 was the first of five red-white-and-blues painted by the Santa Fe, the most of any American railroad. That same day, a more conventional set of SD45s and SD45-2s in the "old" blue and yellow is pictured, below left, climbing eastward through Cajon. At right, in July 1969, an Alco DL600B "Alligator" is leading a mixed set of EMDs starting downhill at Summit, atop Cajon Pass. The Santa Fe DL600Bs were among the very first locomotives to introduce the low nose to American hood units back in 1959.

Below, in the arid Peloncillo Mountains on the Arizona–New Mexico state line just west of San Simon, Ariz., we have a transcontinental encounter on the Southern Pacific main line in early November 1971. With a Baltimore & Ohio GP40 in the lead, an eastbound freight is in the siding to let a fast westbounder through with an SP SD45 on the point. The B&O unit is getting a look at the Wild West through a pool arrangement at St. Louis that resulted in SP units visiting Cumberland, Md., and, as evidenced here, B&O units getting to California. (*Left page,* DONAHUE; *right page,* BOYD)

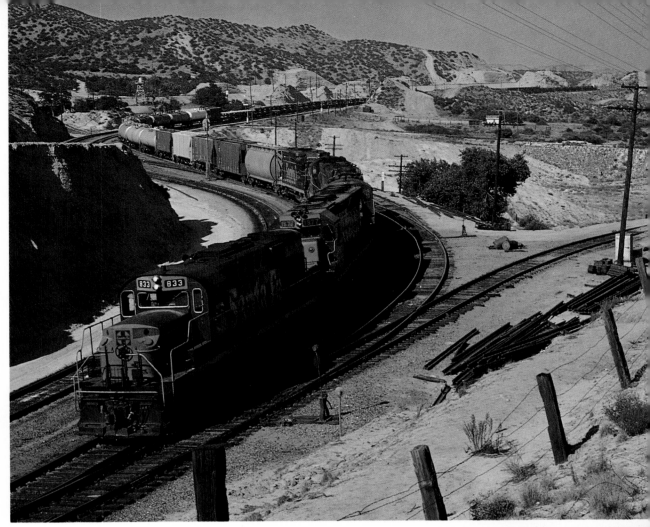

Land of contrasts. At upper left, the classic A-B-B-A set of Santa Fe warbonnets cant into a curve near Navajo, N. Mex., heading Santa Fe's pride and showpiece, the *Super Chief,* westbound in October 1960. The temperature on the desert is over 100 degrees, but inside the elegant all-Pullman train, the passengers are in a state of tranquility, as the Santa Fe "delivers the Southwest to their windows." Inside the *Super*'s cars the traditional Santa Fe Indian décor blends beautifully with the scenery. What better time to be up in the Pleasure Dome looking for Wagon Mound or Haystack Mesa; or in the Turquoise Room for a private gathering amidst Navajo sand paintings and Zuñi hand-fashioned silver splendor. This is Santa Fe's finest stage! At left, and cast against the stark Superstitions, Magma Arizona's train from Superior to Magma heads through the desert under the care of 2-6-0 #6 on February 10, 1960. Although the little Mogul would be retired in a year, the railroad would continue with steam until August 22, 1968. Above, Black Mesa & Lake Powell's three E60Cs head coal from Black Mesa, Ariz., to the power-generating plant at Page in October 1977. This 50,000-volt automated electric railroad may just be the prototype for future railroads. At right, National Railroad of Mexico's sharp-looking 1310-h.p. EMD G12 diesel heads a northbound passenger train out of the tunnel at Lecheria in March 1962. (*Magma Arizona,* BALL; *all others,* DONAHUE)

During the last half of 1974 and well into 1975, I was a regular "cross-county California commuter" while building the American Freedom Train in Oroville and Richmond. I

Driving toward Richmond, I decided to photograph a couple of Southern Pacific commutes. I pulled off Route 101 on the Brisbane City line and set up. Within minutes, a forgotten but familiar harmonic throb of an approaching Fairbanks-Morse Train Master was heard. The big 2400-h.p. engine raced out from under Highway 101 moving a meager three-car commute south. I'd forgotten the FM was a full five years ahead of everybody else with a high-horsepower diesel…I'd forgotten the headlines demonstrators TM-1 thru TM-4 had made way back in 1953—and I did not realize #3021 had once been the TM-4. She still seemed in style and was certainly well worth the trackside diversion.

I realized that this huge locomotive caught between the last of the first-generation diesels and the first of the second-generation diesels was perishing of its own uniqueness. (BALL)

APPENDIX:
THE DIESEL'S STORY

THIS BOOK focuses on the modern era, the 1960s and 1970s, and it is impossible to discuss American railroading and its motive power without getting into the technical jargon of the diesel age. Terms like *Geep*, *Alco*, *H12-44*, *567C*, and *road switcher* are part of the natural language used in describing the hardware, but this can be incomprehensible jibberish to the uninitiated. To make the terminology more understandable, let's take a look at the development and nomenclature of the diesel locomotive.

To appreciate how the diesel fit into the railroad world, it is convenient to start in the 1920s. Steam ruled the rails, and the greatest advances in steam design were still on the drawing boards. A network of streetcars and interurban lines laced both the metropolitan and rural areas of the country, and the technology of electric rail propulsion was reasonably well established. In a small office in Cleveland, Ohio, in 1924, a fledgling business calling itself the Electro-Motive Company was combining a car body from a trolley manufacturer with a six-cylinder 175-h.p. gasoline engine from Winton Engine Co. and electrical equipment from General Electric to produce a self-propelled rail passenger car. The concept was not new, but few of the earlier motor cars were powerful or reliable enough to be categorized as successes. General Electric had pioneered in rail motor car development around the turn of the century, and although it had either solved or was on the right track to solving most of the technological problems, it abandoned the field in 1910.

The basic operating principle of the gas-electric motor car was the use of a large gasoline engine to drive a generator, which supplied electricity to power "traction motors" on the wheels. The Electro-Motive Company's combination was sufficiently successful for over 400 of its "doodlebugs" to be built over the next decade, and a few of them survived in service into the early 1960s. The GM&O car on page 169, typical of the EMC design, was built in January 1928.

At the time when EMC was getting started building its motor cars, the giants of the locomotive business were the "Big Three" steam builders: the American Locomotive Company (Alco), Baldwin, and Lima. No one would have guessed that the little outfit in Cleveland would have them all out of the locomotive business within 50 years. One story, fondly told, is of the stenographer who worked for EMC for half a day in its Cleveland office and left at noon without even accepting her pay, observing that "these blue-sky companies start and fizzle out in no time," and that her boss, Mr. Hamilton, would probably need the money.

In 1930 the General Motors Corporation purchased both EMC and the Winton Engine Company. Thus, both were able to weather the Great Depression with minimal distress. In 1934 the companies made their bid for greatness when Winton supplied a V-12 gas engine for the Union Pacific's *City of Salina* articulated streamliner, and only months later made real history with a two-cycle eight-cylinder diesel engine, the Winton 201A, for the Burlington's #9900 *Zephyr*. Both of these lightweight streamliners used the same drive principle as EMC's gas-electrics: an "oil" engine turning a generator which supplied electricity to traction motors on the wheels.

While it was the streamliners that were gathering the glamour, the true destiny of the internal combustion engine on the railroad was being worked out in homely little rivet-laden boxcab switch engines that were beginning to find their way into industrial areas and special railroad situations where steam locomotives were a problem. America's first commercially produced diesel-electric locomotive, Jersey Central's 300-h.p. boxcab switcher #1000, was turned out in 1925 as a joint venture among Alco, General Electric, and Ingersol-Rand. It's important to note that even at this early date, steam-builder Alco was taking a very active part in diesel locomotive development, and the Alco-GE-IR units of the late 1920s became America's first standardized line of off-the-shelf diesel locomotives. Furthering its commitment to the diesel in 1929, Alco purchased the McIntosh & Seymour Engine Company, acquiring "its own" diesel-engine capability and abandoning the Ingersol-Rand diesel engine of the earlier units but retaining its partnership with GE for electrical equipment. Ironically, GE, with its extensive experience in building electric locomotives both for trolley lines and railroads, was also producing a variety of primitive diesel switching locomotives, using engines of other manufacturers. Whereas the steam builders would custom design almost every locomotive for the specific customer, even the early diesel manufacturers recognized that their locomotives could be marketed as standardized, mass-produced units.

While Winton's 201A diesel engine was going into a number of custom-built streamliners throughout the mid-1930s, EMC could see that the real market was in producing standardized locomotives much as GE and Alco were doing, and in 1934 EMC took its big step in that direction by opening up an expansive new factory in La Grange, Ill. EMC's first off-the-shelf production unit from the La Grange plant was Santa Fe 600-h.p. "SC" #2301 in May 1936. Although it is a slightly newer model, B&M NW2 #1202 on page 28 is very similar to that original SC.

Since Also was primarily in the business of building large steam locomotives, it was not particularly aggressive in developing a road freight or passenger diesel. But since EMC had no such conflict of interest, it made great strides in both areas very rapidly. Planting a pair of its 900-h.p. Winton 201A V-12s in a sleekly styled car body (roughly similar to Illinois Central #4003 on page 155), EMC produced in 1937 its first passenger "E units." With its mid-1930s units, EMC used a horsepower code for assigning model labels: the SC switcher was Six-hundred horsepower with a Cast frame, and the original NW switcher had Nine-hundred horsepower with a Welded frame. Thus, the EA designation for passenger units was derived from Eighteen-hundred horsepower and "A" unit car body, as compared to the "B" unit booster. Subsequent models were identified by combining numbers with the letters, such as the NW, NW1, and NW2 switchers and the E1A, E1B, E2A, and E2B passenger cabs and boosters. The Santa Fe units on page 198 and CGW units on page 150 are good examples of cab and booster-unit combinations.

Let's break away from the locomotive-development chronology for a moment to look at the two primary types of diesels, the four-cycle and two-cycle engines. Both types have the same general physical arrangement, much like typical automobile engines. They have a crankshaft at the bottom churning around in an oil bath with cylinders and pistons positioned above in quantities ranging from six to 20 and in V or inline arrangements. The common diesels of the 1930s were Alco's four-cycle inline six and EMC's Winton two-cycle V-12.

The four-cycle diesel is very similar in function to a modern gasoline engine, except that it replaces the carburetor and spark plug with a mechanical fuel injector. Each cylinder contains one piston and has no openings in the cylinder walls. All valves and the fuel injector are mounted in the head—top—of the cylinder. The "events" in the cylinder as the crank turns are as follows: (1) Intake downstroke: intake valves are open and clean air is drawn or forced into the cylinder. (2) Compression upstroke: all valves are closed and the piston compresses its charge of air, heating it to a very high temperature. (3) Power downstroke: the injector sprays a mist of fuel into the hot, compressed air and the fuel explodes, driving the piston downward, providing the power to turn the crankshaft. (4) Exhaust upstroke: exhaust valves are opened and the upward thrusting piston drives the spent air and combustion gases into the exhaust manifold and out the stack.

A two-cycle diesel is different in that it provides a power thrust on every downstroke. This is accomplished by placing air intake ports near the bottom of the cylinder and keeping the exhaust valves and injector in the head. The events in a two-cycle cylinder are as follows: (1) Nearing the bottom of a power downstroke, the piston uncovers the air intake ports just as the exhaust valves in the head open. High-pressure air is forced into the bottom of the cylinder above the piston, and this fresh charge of air drives the spent air and combustion gases out the exhaust valves at the top. As the crankshaft rotates past bottom dead center, the piston moves upward, covering the air intake ports as the exhaust valves close. The fresh air is now trapped in the cylinder and is compressed and heated by the compression upstroke. (2) Just past top center the injector sprays fuel into the cylinder and, ignited by the air temperature, it explodes and drives the piston downward in the power stroke. Nearing the bottom of the power stroke, the piston uncovers the air intake ports and the whole process repeats itself with every revolution of the crank.

Both the two-cycle and four-cycle diesels used in North America today are powerful, reliable, and rugged. Their horsepower is increased by adding cylinders, by increasing the rpms, and by turbocharging. The basic diesels that were developed in the late 1930s are still in use today and have been improved and upgraded to provide outputs ranging from 600 to 4,200 horsepower. Typical maximum running speeds range from 700 to 1,100 rpm.

Getting back to the late 1930s, EMC was working to put itself into the locomotive business totally independent of any other supplier of major components. While the Winton 201A had proven that the two-cycle engine would work in locomotives, it had its drawbacks and was not well suited to mass production. In 1938 EMC introduced its own diesel engine: the 567. Based upon the Winton 201A, this new engine was designed from the ground up to be a locomotive diesel that could be standardized in both production and application. The 567 was derived from its 567-cubic-inch displacement *per cylinder*. Initially produced in three sizes (a 600-h.p. V-6, 1,000-h.p. V-12, and 1,350-h.p. V-16), the 567 had ample room for growth and would serve EMC for the next 28 years! Simultaneously with the introduction of the 567, EMC began full production at La Grange of all of its major electrical gear (its first production traction motor was a virtual copy of the model 716 motor GE had been supplying up to that point). With its fully independent manufacturing capability, EMC now began to go after a railroad industry full of steam locomotives. The first mass-production road units to receive the new 567 diesel were the 2,000-h.p. passenger E3s and E4s (again, almost identical in appearance to the ICRR #4003 on page 155). Carrying two 1,000-h.p. V-12s and riding six-wheel trucks, the "Es" set the pattern for virtually all EMC passenger diesels that followed. At about the same time, Alco was using the same basic design formula to produce its own standard passenger diesel, the DL109. Uniquely styled by Otto Kuhler, with an angular nose, as seen on Rock Island #621 on page 138, they provided EMC's only nonsteam competition until after World War II.

A word is in order here about trucks. In railroad terminology a *truck* is a wheel assembly; the British call them *bogies*. Diesel trucks are identified with the same number and letter code that had been worked out years earlier for electric locomotives. Letters indicate motors on axles: A is one motor on one axle, B is two motors on two axles, C is three motors on three axles, and D is four motors on four axles. A nonpowered axle used in combination with these is indicated by a number: 1 for one, 2 for two, etc. The most common trucks used under diesel locomotives are the "B" two-axle two-motor truck, and the "C" three-axle three-motor truck. Passenger units such as EMD's Es and Alco's DL109s ride on three-axle two-motor trucks, with the middle axle being an unpowered "idler" to improve the ride; this is designated as an A1A truck. Truck combinations under a locomotive are combined with hyphens, such as B-B or A1A-A1A.

While both EMC and Alco were going for the glory of producing passenger diesels, the real market was freight, and in November 1939 EMC introduced America's first true road freight diesel. Packing a single 1,350-h.p. 567 V-16 into a car body considerably shorter than the Es and riding on a pair of B trucks, the FT carried all of its weight on its drivers and set the format for freight diesels for the next two decades. A somewhat weather-weary FT appears on page 118.

How could a 1,350-h.p. diesel compete with a huge steam 4-8-4 rated at 6,000-h.p.? The answer is essentially in the electrical system. First of all, a diesel-electric locomotive is controlled electrically, and these controls are nearly all standard from one unit to the next. Thus, diesels can be coupled together and linked up with electrical "jumper cables" to permit the engineer in the lead unit to control an entire coupled set of diesels as one locomotive. (Although generally removed when not in use, a jumper cable can be seen on the Milwaukee Road 546 on page 152. The jumper cable is coiled around one of the front handrail stanchions; it plugs into a capped receptacle that is visible on the end view of almost all diesels. All those hoses on either side of the couplers, however, are air lines for the brakes and sanding systems.)

Using its multiple unit—or "m.u."—capability, a single 1,350-h.p. FT could be combined into a four-unit 5,400-h.p. locomotive that would be a match for almost any steamer. Additionally, because of the physics of its directly geared electric-motor drive system, a diesel locomotive can derive its greatest power at low speeds, whereas a steam locomotive is at its greatest disadvantage at low speeds. In starting a train or struggling on a grade, a steam locomotive becomes less capable as it slows or stalls, whereas a diesel becomes more effective as the speed slows.

Probably the diesel's most significant advantage over a steam engine, however, is that it is an "automatic" locomotive. A steam locomotive must be carefully run and knowledgeably fired to make it perform, and its fuel and water supplies must be closely monitored. It requires an incredible amount of manpower to have it cleaned, lubricated, supplied with fuel and water, and kept running. A diesel, on the other hand, will simply "go" when you pull back on the throttle, like your automobile, and its fuel supply is often enough to last for days. It can be left idling unattended or can be shut down completely by the engineer himself. It can be restarted almost instantly—compared with the one to eight hours required to bring up a steam locomotive, depending upon whether or not it has been cold or on standby steam and the condition of its fire.

The diesel's potential for 24-hour-a-day service, rather than its speed, power, or over-the-road capabilities, is what gave it the overwhelming advantage against the steam locomotive. It's significant to observe that in the late 1950s the Illinois Central replaced about 1,000 steam locomotives with roughly 650 diesels—and it would take two 1,500-h.p. diesels to equal one 2-8-2 in pulling power on a road freight. Thus, arguing the specific over-the-road performance capabilities of steam versus diesel is relatively pointless; both could do an excellent job of rolling the boxcars, but the diesel could do it for a longer period of time and with much less manpower overall.

Needless to say, the FT caused quite a stir in 1940 as it traveled the country on a demonstration tour as a four-unit 5,400-h.p. set. The FT proved it could do the job, but the expected time period for competition and acceptance was accelerated greatly by the events of December 7, 1941, and the sudden war emergency. The Electro-Motive Corporation had been merged into General Motors on January 1, 1941, and thanks to the success of the FT demonstrator team, the new GM Electro-Motive Division—EMD—was given the full war-time allotment for construction of diesel freight locomotives by the War Productions Board. This action severely crippled Alco's postwar efforts in the freight-diesel business, because its freight test units were frozen in development during the war as Alco was assigned production on switch engines along with fellow steam builder Baldwin, which had just entered the diesel market with a four-cycle switcher of its own. EMD produced a total of 1,095 FTs before it was replaced in 1946 by the much improved F2. Its diesel competitors would never catch up.

The postwar years were the glory ones for the diesel. They met and vanquished the steam locomotive all across the country. EMD's 1,500-h.p. F3 of 1946 became the locomotive against which all others would be measured, and its 2,000-h.p. E7 headed up passenger trains in every corner of the country (GM&O #884-A on page 140 and KCS #51 on page 173 are F3s, while B&M #3803 on page 29 and GM&O #103-A on page 169 are E7s). Alco got into the freight-unit business in 1945 with its 1,500-h.p. FA1 (GM&O #728 on page 119 was one of the first), and Baldwin jumped in in 1947 with its DR4-4-1500 "Babyface" units (CNJ #77 on page 74). Tending to customize more than standardize—as was the tradition in steam-locomotive construction—Baldwin built a few unique passenger units as well.

Alco introduced its successful and remarkably handsome "2,000-h.p. passenger diesels," subsequently dubbed "PAs," in 1946 (see Santa Fe #61 on page 136 and D&H #18 and #19 on page 31). The massive-looking Alco PAs used a single four-cycle model-244 V-16 engine in its passenger units, whereas EMD was using two 567 V-12s for the same horsepower output. The one feature that all passenger units of the era had in common was the A1A truck. A number of roads disliked the idea of the idler wheels and opted for high-geared freight Fs for passenger service—the Santa Fe on page 198, CN and CP on page 193, and NP on page 149 are notable examples of this. Some Fs were made a few feet longer to accommodate a steam generator and its water supply used to heat the passenger cars, and these were designated "FPs," like CPR FP7 #1400 on page 193.

Less than a year prior to World War II, Alco had developed a novel concept in a freight locomotive, but its full significance would not be appreciated until almost a decade later. Taking its basic 1,000-h.p. switch engine (such as Long Island 443 on page 39), Alco lengthened its frame, added a short hood behind the cab, and put the whole thing on road trucks. In its "RS1" (pictured on page 26 as GMR #405), Alco had created the first road switcher, a locomotive so successful and versatile that all RS1s built prior to the war were confiscated by the U.S. Army for use overseas. Production resumed after the war, and the RS1 remained in production essentially unchanged for 17 years, the longest production run for any American diesel locomotive model. In 1946, without discontinuing its 1,000-h.p. RS1, Alco went for a full-horsepower road switcher in its RS2, which at 1,500-h.p. was competitive with any road freight unit at the time. (Monon #23 on page 134 is an RS2.)

Seeing the success Alco was having with its RS1 and RS2, EMD tried to crossbreed the road switcher with a conventional F unit and came up with its strange "branchline locomotive" BL2 (see BAR BL2s #51 and #56 on page 16). The BL2 sold quite a number of units, but its concept was definitely a failure and was never repeated. The main problem with the BL2 is that it retained the "bridge truss" construction of the F unit rather than adopting the "girder frame" of the switch engine and road switcher. On an F unit—or any other "covered wagon" unit like the EMD Es or Alco FAs and PAs—the side wall of the car body is built like a truss bridge that supports the roof while it gives rigidity to the underframe.

The problem with the side-truss construction is that it boxes in the engine compartment, making access to the engine difficult through roof hatches or in the narrow aisleways inside the body. A road switcher or switch engine, on the other hand, carries all its strength in its underframe, like a flatcar, with its narrow hoods merely acting as a cover over the innards—and with lots of foldaway doors on the sides for easy access. While the BL2 solved the F unit's problem of rearward visibility, its trusswork construction still left it difficult to work on in the engineroom. Something better was needed.

In October 1949 EMD introduced the answer: the GP7 (BAR #70 on page 17, PRR #8551 on page 134, and BN #1574 on page 157). Packing the same 1,500-h.p. 567B V-16 engine as its "covered wagon" twin F7, the GP7 was identical to the F7 in every respect except car-body style. Like Alco's RS1 and RS2, it was the diesel in dungarees. The versatility and bi-directional capability of the road switcher, combined with its accessibility for ease of maintenance, quickly made it the most popular style of locomotive on American rails. Initially designed to be severe in outline and sufficiently unattractive to present little competition to EMD's already established line of handsome "covered wagon" freight and passenger units, the GP7 turned out to have a classic beauty born of functionalism that was to render it possibly the most enduring of all diesel locomotive designs. The "GP" designation, standing for General Purpose, was almost immediately colloquially distorted into "Geep," and railroading got a new and universally accepted name.

As EMD was establishing its position as the nation's largest diesel locomotive builder, its competition was not standing still. World War II had proven the diesel's superiority, and the steam-locomotive builders could see the end of their traditional product. All made an attempt, one way or another, to get into the diesel game. Alco was by far the strongest and, in partnership with GE, was firmly in second place. Baldwin Locomotive Works, which had been well established with Westinghouse, building electric locomotives for decades, started producing diesel switchers just before the outbreak of the war. Of the Big Three steam builders, only Lima held out, proclaiming in trade advertisements throughout the late 1940s that "there is still a place for the truly modern steam locomotive in the United States." But with the construction of its last steam locomotive, Nickel Plate Road 2-8-4 #779 in 1949, even Lima had to start building diesel switchers to survive in the railroad marketplace. (NKP 2-8-4 #759 on pages 25 and 104 is virtually identical to #779.)

In 1944 a new company entered the locomotive business. The Fairbanks-Morse Company of Chicago, known generally as a manufacturer of heavy-duty scales and industrial hardware, had developed an unusual opposed-piston diesel engine which had proven very successful in submarines. With its "o.p." engine first applied to a rail vehicle in six passenger motor cars in 1939, FM entered the market on a full scale in 1944 with a 1,000-h.p. switch engine and followed up with a road switcher in 1947 (Milwaukee Road #428 on page 152 is a slightly later version of the FM road switcher). The FM factory was located in Beloit, Wis.

The FM opposed-piston engine was unique in the railroad field. Basically a two-cycle like EMD's, the FM engine had no head on its cylinders but had a crankshaft on both top and bottom. Each cylinder contained two pistons, one reaching in from the top and one from the bottom, with the injector in the middle. As the geared crankshafts turned, the pistons would thrust inward simultaneously and then power outward together as the fuel was burned. Smooth-running and very powerful, the FM o.p. had greater output potential than any of its contemporaries, but its two crankshafts made it very difficult to maintain. FM sold a surprising number of switchers, road switchers, and cab units in the late 1940s and early 1950s with six- to 12-cylinder models ranging in horsepower from 1,000 to 2,400. Milwaukee Road #23C on page 150 is an eight-cylinder 1,600-h.p. FM "C-liner" cab unit. The C-liner of 1950 and Baldwin "Sharknose" of 1949 were probably the last new stylings of the traditional "covered wagon" car body. The future belonged to the road switcher. (D&H #1205 on page 57 is a Baldwin "Shark.")

In 1948 Baldwin introduced the last significant concept in diesel locomotive design: the six-motor road switcher. By going to the C-C wheel arrangement, the low-speed "lugging" capability of a diesel locomotive was dramatically increased. Baldwin's six-motor road switcher is typified by Milwaukee Road #564 on page 151. Alco quickly followed suit by putting C trucks under its RS3 in 1950, creating an RSD4 like Utah #304 and #305 on page 191. FM built its first C-C in 1951, and EMD produced the definitive machine in 1952 with its SD7, similar to the DM&IR SD9s #130 and #104 on page 145. All of these six-motors were in the 1,500-to-1,800-horsepower range until FM upped the ante to 2,400 horsepower with its brutish Train Master in 1953 (see SP #3021 on page 200).

The 1950s saw the steam-versus-diesel conflict fought to its conclusion, and steam was vanquished. The diesels that did it were the streamlined passenger and freight cab units, switchers, road switchers, and six-motor units manufactured roughly 65 percent by EMD, 25 percent by Alco, and 10 percent by Baldwin, FM and Lima combined. Of these warriors, EMD and FM units hummed with the smooth sound of two-cycle engines, while Alco, Baldwin, and Lima beat out a chugging rhythm with their four-cycle power plants. Each acquired its own personality. The EMDs were smooth and confident, all business but rather "plain vanilla"—except for the beautiful chant of its twin-engined E units, probably the most richly pleasant-sounding of all diesel locomotives. FMs tended to drum contentedly and emit profuse clouds of blue smoke when started up or suddenly accelerated. The lumbering four-cycle Baldwins had a thundering and pounding beat, and the Baldwins achieved a reputation as tremendous low-speed luggers thanks to their massive and almost indestructible Westinghouse traction motors. Alcos, however, were the favorites of the train watchers; their galloping beat and whistling turbochargers were entertaining even when idling, as they'd seem to falter almost to a stall before rebounding with a resurgence of life as the governor linkage caught up its slack. The Alcos would emit great billows of black smoke while accelerating and blow red flames from their stacks when working wide open. No real match for the smoky and noisy drama of the steam locomotives they were displacing, the "first generation" diesels of the 1950s soon revealed a charm all their own. And the brilliant colors that adorned their slab-sided flanks and interestingly styled contours brought a fresh brightness to the sooty railroad scene.

As the last steam locomotives were being rooted out of their final strongholds, the "second generation" of diesels was about to hasten the retirement of the prewar and early postwar units. In an effort to produce a locomotive competitive with FM's 2,400-h.p. Train Master of 1953, both EMD and Alco boosted their biggest six-motor units to the 2,400-h.p. range in the late 1950s, and the horsepower race was under way. The B&LE 2,400-h.p. Alco DL600 #885 on page 92 is one of those units.

EMD's application of a turbocharger to its 16-cylinder 567 to boost its output from 1,800 to 2,400 horsepower is generally regarded as the first tentative step into dieseldom's second generation. At the same time came a change that was to characterize almost all diesels from 1960 on: the chop-nose or low short hood. From its inception, the road switcher had been a bi-directional machine, and the first such units, Alco's RS1s and RS2s, carried on the steam tradition by putting the cab at the rear, a position favored by many engine crewmen who felt more secure with that long hood out front to act as a battering ram in case of accident. But the EMD Geep was introduced with the short hood as the front, considering visibility more important. Most railroads went along with the short-end-forward policy, but it was optional to have the controls reversed to make the long hood forward—the "front" of a unit is determined by the arrangement of the control stand in the cab which places the engineer on the right side facing forward. Many railroads, mostly Eastern, opted to run their Geeps long end forward, as exemplified by the CV #4551 on page 28, NYC #5698 on page 53, and Conrail #7189 on page 76. Virtually all Alco road switchers were built with long end forward, but some roads, like the TP&W on page 158, rebuilt them to run short end forward.

The lowering of the short hood and placing of a windshield on that end of the cab pretty well resolved the matter of the short end being front, although some roads like the Norfolk & Western and Southern persisted in retaining the high short hood and running long end forward—see N&W on pages 103 and 107.

The first diesels to get factory-chopped short hoods were SD24s and Alco DL600Bs for the Santa Fe in 1959; Santa Fe Alco #833 on page 197 is one of these. The horsepower race heated up rapidly in the next few years, with EMD jacking up the horsepower of its basic 1,750-h.p. Geep to 2,000 with the GP20 of 1959, 2,250 with the GP30 of 1961, and 2,500 with the GP35 of 1963 (the GP20 is very similar to the NYS&W GP18 #1804 on page 74, while C&NW #820 on page 153 is a GP30, and WP #3012 on page 195 is a GP35). By 1963 three of the postwar diesel manufacturers had quit the market: Lima went out by merging with Baldwin in 1951, and Baldwin itself exited in 1956. Fairbanks-Morse was the next to go in 1963. This should have left EMD and Alco alone to fight it out, but a new factor was making itself felt. General Electric decided in the late 1950s to get into the road locomotive market on its own, instead of just supplying electrical equipment to Alco. In 1960 it introduced the U25B, the first true second-generation diesel designed from the ground up. The Erie Lackawanna unit trailing on page 90 is a U25B.

Adapting the Cooper-Bessemer four-cycle turbocharged "FDL-16" V-16 diesel to its technical and manufacturing needs at a rating of 2,500 h.p., GE got a 500-h.p. jump on EMD in the B-B hood unit format that was proving by far to be the most popular with the railroads. The U25B incorporated design simplifications that would revise the thinking of the entire industry.

The U25B introduced self-cleaning inertial filters to replace the messy oil-soaked fiber filters that hid behind the louvers on virtually every diesel built since the 1930s, and it replaced the four or more individual motor-and-fan traction motor blowers with one big blower driven directly off the engine. In addition, it slightly pressurized the engineroom and electrical cabinets to keep road dirt from entering these important working areas. These and other improvements introduced on the U25B were incorporated in the designs of most EMD and Alco units which followed.

Recovering from the corporate shock that its steam locomotive business was indeed dead, Alco began development of its new "251" model diesel engine—in Alco's parlance, the "2" was its code number for its 9″ x 10½″ cylinder size, and the "51" indicated the year it was first tested. The 251 was a rugged machine with plenty of room for growth; it became the standard around which Alco built its locomotives from the early 1950s onward. The

1,800-h.p. RS11 displaced the RS3 in 1956 as Alco's standard B-B road switcher, and the RS3's smoothly curved lines (WM #190 on page 94) gave way to a boxy car body with distinctively notched ends (similar to PRR DL600 #8657 on page 89). The 1,800-h.p. DL702 became Alco's six-motor version of the RS11 (C&O #2016 on page 110 is a DL702).

Alco's second-generation units were its "Century series" of the early 1960s. The 12-cylinder 2,000-h.p. C420 (Century unit with 4 motors and 2000 horsepower), 16-cylinder 2,400-h.p. C424 and 16-cylinder six-motor 2,750-h.p. C628 of 1963 became Alco's most competitive models. (L&HR units on pages 62 and 63 are C420s, while LV #632 on page 59 is a C628.) A year later Alco put the same big GE generator that GE was using in its own U25B into the C424 and upped its horsepower to 2,500, creating the C425 (PRR #2432 on page 130 is a C425). Alco, at this time, was still technically Alco-GE, producing locomotives in partnership with GE, which was supplying the electrical equipment. With GE in the market on its own, it was evident that Alco was about to be in for some interesting competition.

With complex but standardized locomotives being manufactured by corporate giants, it's not surprising that there are few individuals who can be identified as having contributed in a noticeable way to the development of the diesel locomotive. One notable exception to this situation, however, was David S. Neuhart, the man who became the top mechanical officer of the Union Pacific Railroad in 1949. Dave Neuhart wanted truly big locomotives—as would befit the man whose department operated the world's largest steam locomotives. He encouraged GE's experiments with gas-turbine-electric locomotives, a program which resulted in the awesome 8,500-h.p. UP turbines of 1958 (see turbine #16 on page 188), which Neuhart subsequently boosted to 10,000 horsepower!

Dave Neuhart and his team in Omaha came up with an idea for a super diesel locomotive, and by 1963 had Alco, GE, and EMD each building their own versions of his machine. With typical units of the time producing 2,500 h.p., Neuhart proposed putting two such diesel engines on one frame and grouping four two-motor trucks under the unit to apply the power. Both Alco and GE came up with mechanically similar machines that were quite different in appearance. The Alco Century 855 (UP #61, page 188) packed two V-16 2,750-h.p. 251 engines for a total output of 5,500 h.p. into a hood car body with a more or less typical cab and short hood. The GE U50, however, placing two V-16 2,500-h.p. diesels into a similar car body for an output of 5,000 h.p., was uniquely styled with a broadly rounded full-width nose and high windshields (UP #45 on page 178). While GE and Alco used four individual two-motor trucks connected by span bolsters, EMD came up with its DD35 by putting two 2,500-h.p. turbocharged 567 power plants into the unit which rode on one pair of gigantic four-axle four-motor "D" trucks (these are seen under the even bigger and newer DDA40X #6900 on page 189).

Of the three "double diesels" of 1963, the EMD was the most successful, resulting in two subsequent models in following years—the DD35A and DDA40X. The latter, built in 1969, will probably go down as the all-time largest diesel-electric ever built, at 6,600-h.p. (UP #6900 on page 189). The GE U50 was also a successful unit, 23 of which went to the UP and three to the Southern Pacific. In 1969 GE produced a similar U50C, pulling the same horsepower out of two V-12s—instead of the V-16s on the original U50s—and riding on C-C trucks (UP #5033 and #5010 on pages 178–179). Only the Alco C855, of which two cabs and one booster were produced, was not duplicated. Dave Neuhart died in 1973, leaving a legacy of an entire fleet of the largest diesel locomotives the world is ever likely to see. Ironically, by the end of 1979 only the EMD DD35s and DDA40Xs survive of all Neuhart's turbines and double diesels.

Getting back to the horsepower race of the early 1960s that spawned the UP giants, EMD, Alco, and GE were all competing neck and neck with 2,500-h.p. units in both B-B and C-C configurations. The first victim of the struggle was Alco. Dependent upon now-rival GE for electrical technology and hardware, the last of the steam builders was at a distinct disadvantage. Undergoing corporate convulsions in the mid-1960s, Alco produced its last domestic locomotive in 1968 and withdrew to its former Montreal Locomotive Works subsidiary in Canada, where it thrives to this day as Canada's number two locomotive builder. General Motors has its EMD subsidiary General Motors Diesel Ltd. (GMD) in London, Ontario, and is presently Canada's largest locomotive builder. Interestingly, GE does not produce locomotives in Canada, but leaves that market to its old partner Alco, owned today by Bombardier, Ltd., better known as a manufacturer of snowmobiles.

With Alco out of the way, it was left to EMD and GE to fight it out. The GE FDL-16 diesel was brand new and had lots of growing room, but EMD's trusty 1939-vintage 567 had been speeded up and turbocharged to about the limit of its capacity. By retaining the same external dimensions and crankshaft but narrowing the thickness of the water jacket surrounding its cylinders, EMD was able to increase the inside diameter of its cylinders to produce a 645-cubic-inch displacement. The new "645" engine was mated up to an AC alternator instead of a DC generator to form the basis of EMD's new "40 series" units in 1965. The alternator had a distinct advantage over a generator, and a bank of solid-state diodes—transistors that resemble slightly overgrown spark plugs—was used to rectify the alternator's AC output to DC for the traction motors. EMD now had an engine that could compete with GE on an equal footing.

Prior to 1965, the largest number of cylinders ever applied successfully to a single crankshaft was 16, but using a computer to work out the stresses and firing order, EMD built a huge 20-cylinder version of its new 645, packing 3,600 horsepower. Introduced in a series of demonstrator units in 1965, EMD's new "SD45" was the immediate king of the road. (SD45 demonstrator #4353 is shown on the D&H on page 57, and Santa Fe #5508 and SP #9032 on pages 196–197 are typical SD45s.)

GE answered by tweaking its 16-cylinder FDL-16 up to 3,600 h.p. and putting it on the road in both a six-motor and four-motor version. The middle unit in the Clinchfield set on page 111 is a U36C six-motor, and the Auto-Train units on page 99 are four-motor U36Bs. (GE identified its locomotives as the "Universal" series, and its terminology, U36B indicated Universal, 3600-h.p., B trucks. The units picked up the nickname "U-boat.") The horsepower race had reached the plateau in 1971 that it would retain for the rest of the decade. Instead of horsepower, the emphasis in the 1970s would be on reliability, and the changes would be subtle and evolutionary rather than dramatic and revolutionary. Only the boxy "cowl" car body of certain passenger and freight units and Amtrak's SDP40Fs (see Amtrak 515 on page 181) would introduce a truly new face.

Not everyone wanted the highest-horsepower top-of-the-line units, and throughout the 1970s EMD turbocharged 3,000-h.p. four-motor GP40 and six-motor SD40s were top sellers along with its nonturbocharged 2,000-h.p. GP38. Modular solid-state control circuitry and reliability improvements prompted EMD's "Dash-Two" series in 1972, but none of the models was upped in horsepower at that time. Rock Island #4348 on page 177 is a GP38-2, while B&M #308 on page 21 and Chessie #4239 on page 105 are GP40-2s, and Rock Island #4799 on page 181 is an SD40-2.

By the end of the 1970s EMD and GE were settling down to continued improvement in reliability and a new concern for fuel economy. EMD had about 70 percent of the market and GE 30 percent—interestingly, just about the same proportion as their respective plant capacities. Rebuild shops operated by railroads or outside contractors were creating some new looks on the rails with production upgrading rebuilds of older units, such as Illinois Central's "GP10" #8064 on page 154 and Milwaukee's "SD10" #546 on page 152. The expected economic lifetime of a properly maintained diesel locomotive is about 15 years, after which time it is usually traded back to its manufacturer for a new model or rebuilt and upgraded at home or in a contract shop.

The continuing development of new locomotives, along with the aging and rebuilding or replacement of older units, keeps the railroad motive power scene constantly changing. Combined with mergers among the railroad companies themselves and the changing or elimination of traditional paint schemes, this results in almost any locomotive becoming a "collector's item" within its own lifetime.

As I scan the photos in this book, representative of the past two decades, I am struck with the realization that probably two-thirds of what has been shown is now gone. Within a short time the common becomes the uncommon and then the rare. It is this flow of instant history and the sheer drama of railroading itself that brings kids down to the tracks to watch trains and turns some of them into men with cameras who try to capture moments of the passing scene on film.

Jim Boyd
Newton, New Jersey

INDEX

This index is arranged alphabetically by railroad. Diesel locomotives are identified by builder, model, and road number, where available. Steam locomotives are identified by class where appropriate, wheel arrangement, and road number. Electric locomotives, multiple-unit cars, and motor cars are identified with appropriate data. Page numbers are in italics.

Abbreviations for diesel builders:
Alco: American Locomotive Company, Alco Products. Baldwin: Baldwin Locomotive Works. EMC: Electro-Motive Corporation. EMD: Electro-Motive Division of General Motors. FM: Fairbanks-Morse. GE: General Electric. GMD: General Motors Diesel Limited of Canada.